CONTENTS

1   **Introduction**
What will I learn from this book?..5
How will this book help me?...5
The coursework and the examination...6
NABs...6
The final examination...6
What's in this book? 7
How should I use this book? 8
Command Words..8
Command words in action 10
Focus on the command words...14

2   **Unit Assessments (NABs)**
Introduction..19
Administrative Services NAB...21
Information Technology for Management NAB 22
Practice time..23
Practice NAB 54

3   **The Final Examination**
Introduction...55
Tackling Section 1 57
Tackling Section 2..62
Paper 2...65
Spreadsheets 68
Databases 87
Word processing 100
Conclusion 110

1   Introduction

What will I learn from this book?

How will this book help me?

The coursework and the examination

NABs

The final examination

What's in this book?

How should I use this book?

Command words

Command words in action

Focus on the command words

WHAT WILL I LEARN FROM THIS BOOK?

You will learn about the skills you need to achieve the best possible grade in Higher Administration. You will learn how to answer the type of questions you will be asked in the unit assessments and in the final examination. This book contains suggested solutions and examples, with tips on how to improve your grade.

HOW WILL THIS BOOK HELP ME?

This book will take you through the skills you need for your Higher Administration course stage by stage. There are practice unit assessment questions (referred to as NABs) and you will be given hints, tips and advice on how best to tackle these questions, so that you gain more marks and do well in Higher Administration.

THE COURSEWORK AND THE EXAMINATION

Higher Administration consists of two units:

● Administrative Services
● Information Technology for Management

NABs

There are two internal assessments – or NABs – for the Higher Administration course.

The assessment for **Administrative Services** is a series of short response questions covering the five outcomes, taken under closed book (exam) conditions with a time limit of 1 hour. In order to pass this NAB you must gain at least 60% of the available marks in the assessment.

Information Technology for Management (ITFM) is in two parts.

● **Part 1** is a series of short response questions covering the role of information in decision making and the impact of Information and Communication Technology (ICT) on work practices and management of information. This assessment is also taken under closed book conditions with a time limit of 30 minutes. In order to pass you must gain 60% of the available marks.

● **Part 2** is a practical assignment which includes activities using email, e-diary, presentation software and the internet, as well as spreadsheets, word processing and databases. This assessment is taken in supervised conditions (a teacher is always present), but you will be allowed access to help menus within the software and/or paper-based IT manuals. There is a time limit of 2 hours and 30 minutes. In order to pass you must gain 60% of the available marks in the assessment.

You need to pass both Parts 1 and 2 to gain the ITFM NAB.

See Chapter 2 for more information on internal assessment.

THE FINAL EXAMINATION

You will need to sit this at the end of the course during the SQA exam period (usually in May). The exam is made up of two papers.

Paper	Content	Marks and timing
Paper 1	Has two sections: **Section A** is based on a short case study with questions. There is no choice in this section, so you must complete all of the questions. **Section B** consists of five extended response questions, from which *you must choose two*.	This paper lasts for 1 hour and 20 minutes. Section A is worth 20 marks. Each question in Section B is worth 20 marks. Total available marks for Paper 1 = 60 marks.
Paper 2	This paper consists of a business problem which you need to solve using spreadsheet, word processing and database software, with one of the tasks requiring integration.	This paper lasts for 1 hour and 20 minutes. Total available marks for Paper 2 = 60 marks.

In general if you gain:

70% or more of the marks in the final exam you will get a grade **A** award;
60–69% you will get a grade **B** award;
50–59% you will get a grade **C** award.

See Chapter 3 for more information about the final exam.

You need to pass both the NABs and the final exam to be awarded your Higher Administration.

WHAT'S IN THIS BOOK?

Chapter 1

This chapter provides you with knowledge of the basic skills required to answer the types of questions you will get in the NABs and in the final exam. In particular, it will focus on the use of the 'command' words. Responding correctly to the command words is essential if you hope to get good marks. This section will increase your awareness of what is being asked and how to go about answering questions to boost your chances of gaining full marks.

Chapter 1 will focus on the actual **wording** of questions, which will prepare you for the internal assessment and final examination.

Chapter 2

This chapter looks at the **internal** unit assessments, also known as NABs. You must pass the internal assessments if you are to be awarded an overall grade in Higher Administration.

This chapter will help you prepare using practical examples which cover the areas of assessment. Use this chapter for the end of unit assessments, and also in preparation for the external examination, as the questions are similar to those asked in the exam. Revisiting this chapter before the exam will help you recap on how the command words should affect your answers.

Chapter 3

Here we look at the final examination. This chapter will bring together all the tips you have learned throughout the book to help boost your overall final score. This chapter will focus on exam technique and will show you the best way to tackle questions. It will also show you the standard of work expected for a grade A, B or C.

HOW SHOULD I USE THIS BOOK?

This book can help you at various points in your course. Dip into it at any time – but most importantly, make sure that you come back and study it thoroughly when you prepare for end of unit assessments, prelims and the final exam. That's when you will find that the advice, tips and recommended skills in this book make a real difference to your studies and help boost your grade.

COMMAND WORDS

The questions in Higher Administration use 'command' words.

The **command** word is not something that you can choose to obey or ignore – it is a **demand** to answer the question in a specific way. You must make sure that you understand the differences between the command words. Ignoring the command word and just writing what you know may result in no marks being awarded. The markers are given strict instructions to make sure they mark candidates' answers according to the command word.

A remark on the command words in a recent report:

'... candidates did not show clear understanding of what was required in order to gain marks ...'

SQA External Assessor Report

Underline or highlight the command word(s) used in a question. This will help ensure that you focus on how you should answer the question.

Take your time and read the question carefully. Make sure that your answer relates to what is actually asked, and not just what you *think* is asked.

Here is a list of the command words.

Learn their meanings and use this page when answering questions until you are confident that you know how to respond to the different command words.

Command word	Definitions
Identify or state	These basically mean **name** items or points. These are very simple command words so may only make up part of a question. They will not be worth a lot of marks.
Suggest	This is more than just naming – you will be expected to go on and give an idea or make a recommendation or propose a course of action.
Outline	This calls for you to state the main features. You will be expected to give a number of points but not in great detail – really just a summary. Look at the marks to see how many points you need to give. The greater the number of marks, the more information there has to be in the answer.
Describe	Give an outline as above but in addition give an explanation or an example of what you are talking about.
Discuss	This is where you usually (but not always) need to give advantages and disadvantages, strengths and weaknesses or benefits and drawbacks.
	Your answer must be organised and if possible you should be giving examples to illustrate your answer and show what you mean.
	You might also be asked to give a conclusion or make a recommendation – the mark allocation will give you an idea of how much detail is required.
	You cannot answer a 'discuss' question using a simple list – the points made must be developed and where possible you should give both sides of the argument.

(Continued)

Compare	When comparing, you are expected to show that you understand the similarities and/or differences between different methods/choices. For example:
	*Example 1 and example 2 **are similar** in that they both have …*
	*Example 1 will have … **whereas** example 2 will show …*
	You need to make sure that you make a statement for each mark; you may also have to justify what you have said, or draw a conclusion.
Justify	You must state *why* a course of action has been taken or give good reasons to support a suggestion.

Other terms to be aware of	
Consequence	The consequence of an action is a *direct* result of it.
	For instance, how the issue identified affects the organisation or the employee; what might happen as a direct result of failing to take action or to take account of something.
	A consequence of failing your driving test is that you can't apply for jobs that state you must be able to drive.
Implication	An implication is a *possible* result of an action and is usually *long term*.
	These are the far-reaching effects of a course of action taken by the organisation or employee. There could be many implications – what you have to note is if you are asked to *describe* or *discuss* the implication(s).
	*An **implication** of failing your Higher Administration is that you will have fewer options open to you when you leave school.*

Always look at the marks being awarded to the question – this will give you an idea of how much you have to write. Avoid bulleted lists – these are really not suitable for Higher and you are unlikely to get many, if any, marks if you answer in this way.

COMMAND WORDS IN ACTION

Look at the following examples of command words from recent past papers and note how you need to give different types of answer depending on the command word used. The first two examples both contain the command word 'describe' and are worth 6 marks. You will see you need to make sure that you give detail in your answers.

> Describe ways in which an organisation can prevent
> computer viruses from affecting them.
>
> 6 marks

This question is looking for at least three different ways an organisation can do this; in other words, you will need to **outline a way** and then go on to give **an illustration or an example** of how that method prevents computer viruses. You must also make sure that you give different examples for each point you develop.

Here is a good answer to this question:

 Install antivirus software which will protect your computer [1 mark] and ensure that it is regularly updated. [1 mark]

Install firewalls which are barriers between computers and the web; [1 mark] they help to prevent outside sources such as hackers gaining access to the computer system and data. [1 mark]

Regularly inform staff about the organisation's policies and procedures and give training and demonstrations; [1 mark] this will make staff aware of threats such as emails with attachments from unknown sources or downloading software from the internet. [1 mark]

However, this next question is more specific:

> Describe three consequences and their implications to an
> organisation of inadequate preparation for meetings.
>
> 6 marks

You need to make sure that you do mention three **different** consequences and then **link** the implications to gain full marks in the answer. Just mentioning what will happen if you don't prepare properly for the meeting will not get all the marks.

It might help if you write your answer in two columns – in this way it is easier to see how the consequences and implications are linked.

Consequence	Implication
The venue may have been double-booked or not booked at all. 1 mark	The meeting will need to be postponed, causing inconvenience to attendees. 1 mark
No paperwork sent out in advance, for instance, minutes of the last meeting. 1 mark	Attendees unable to familiarise themselves with topics, so making informed discussion at the meeting difficult. 1 mark
Equipment not booked in time, or not checked before use to ensure it is working. 1 mark	Speaker unable to give a presentation to the meeting, so time wasted. 1 mark

> Justify the expense to an organisation of introducing an intranet.
>
> 4 marks

When you justify something you state **why it is worthwhile**.

Although expensive to implement, an intranet offers several potential benefits that make it worthwhile in the long run.

A good answer is given below.

Internal communication can be improved, as documents can be posted centrally for all staff to access [1 mark] or email can be used to speed up communication between members of staff. [1 mark] Staff will be able to access, process and transmit information quickly – improving efficiency and increasing the amount of work that they can do. [1 mark] Company policies can be held centrally – making it easier to ensure that all staff have access to the same version. [1 mark]

You could also have mentioned:

- Staff can access documents on the intranet from anywhere with an intranet connection (they don't have to be at their own desks) – making them more efficient.
- Improved working practices will make the organisation more competitive.

- Forms and templates can be made available centrally, so all staff have easy access to the most recent versions.
- Details of job vacancies can be posted for all staff to see.
- It is easy to add links from one place to another on the intranet (or internet) so staff can quickly access related information.
- It is quicker and cheaper to distribute updated copies of policies/documents – the intranet copy can be updated and everyone can get access to the updated version without the need to print and distribute copies.

Suggest a way in which each of the following spreadsheet features may be used.

- Comments
- Conditional formatting
- Dynamic linkage
- Named range

4 marks

There are four features and 4 marks available – so you will get 1 mark for a relevant suggestion for each feature. The feature has been named, so you must go on and propose a use for the feature. You are not being asked to *describe* the feature but to suggest what it could be used for.

You will not get more than 1 mark per feature, so there is no point in suggesting lots of uses for one feature and none for another.

 Comments are like electronic post its/stickies and may be used to explain what a value in a cell means. 1 mark

Conditional formatting may be used to draw attention to figures that meet specific criteria, e.g. >=80. 1 mark

Dynamic linkage is used to link a spreadsheet to a word processed document, so that when the spreadsheet is updated the data in the word processed document is updated automatically. 1 mark

Named range may be used instead of cell addresses in formulas and functions, which can make the formula/function easier to understand, e.g. =Basic Pay + Overtime rather than =D4+E4. 1 mark

Any valid suggestion of why the feature would be used would earn a point. You could also give examples of when the feature may be used, as with **conditional formatting** and **named range** above.

You could also have mentioned:

- **Comments** may be used to explain:
  where a figure has come from,
  how a figure has been calculated,
  what your thoughts were when entering something.

- **Dynamic linkage:**
  may be used to link figures or a chart in a presentation file to source data on a worksheet, so that the presentation file is kept up to date with the data in the workbook.

- **Conditional formatting:**
  may be used to draw attention to figures that fall within or outside a certain range so that you can quickly spot figures that differ from what you would normally expect.

- **Named range:**
  may be used to reduce the need for absolute addressing in a formula or function.

Remember!

- The command word is the **instruction** telling you how you will need to answer the question.
- <u>Underline</u> the command word to remind you how you should set out your answer.
- **Always** read the question fully before you start answering.
- **Note** the number of marks that are allocated – and make a point for each one.

See Chapter 3 for more information about the final exam.

FOCUS ON THE COMMAND WORDS

We are now going to look at some questions that focus on the same topic but which use different command words.

The first two examples test knowledge of the working environment.

Type 1 asks for two **consequences** and is worth 4 marks. It will not be enough to simply give two statements in your answer; you will need to **develop** those statements to say what the likely effects will be.

Type 2 is a **justify** question – you will need to give reasons **why it is worthwhile** doing what has been decided. This time you will need to give four different reasons to gain all the marks.

Question type 1

> Describe two possible consequences for the employee moving from a cellular to an open-plan layout. **4 marks**

 If the employee moves from a cellular to an open-plan office then they may find that they are able to communicate more easily with their colleagues, [1 mark] which will lead to greater efficiency. [1 mark] They may have less privacy, [1 mark] which will mean that they will need to be more careful when discussing confidential information or working with confidential papers. [1 mark]

Question type 2

> Justify an organisation's decision to change from an open-plan layout to a traditional cellular layout. **4 marks**

 It may be the case that the organisation has noticed that staff are easily distracted in an open plan office. 1 mark

Holding meetings and finding space to work on confidential matters might be difficult to arrange and a cellular layout is better if the nature of the work requires privacy. 1 mark

Air conditioning and other environmental issues can cause problems in an open-plan layout; if employees are complaining about headaches, colds, being tired etc, it may be due to not being able to control their environment. 1 mark

There tends to be less storage space available in open-plan offices: if the organisation is expanding, staff may find it difficult to store essential files. 1 mark

The next two examples test your knowledge of using different types of software when preparing meetings.

Type 1 is a **discuss** question and is worth 8 marks.

You must discuss at least **three different** software packages to get your marks. When discussing something, don't just suggest what you could use – you must go on and say why it is good or bad, or what the advantages/disadvantages of it might be.

To get the other 2 marks you would either need to discuss a fourth package, or add additional relevant points to one or two of the other three packages.

Type 2 is an **implications** question and is worth 4 marks.

As there are 4 marks, and two examples of software, you should suggest two implications for each example. In this example, an implication is a **possible** result of not using the software suggested.

Question type 1

An administrative assistant will use a variety of software when planning a meeting.

Discuss the use of at least **three** software packages for this purpose.

8 marks

Word processing software, spreadsheet software, email and e-diary software could be used when planning a meeting.

Word processing software could be used to prepare the notice of the meeting, the agenda and the minutes of the previous meeting. The use of this software could speed up the preparation of these documents, as templates could be used. However, staff need to be trained in the use of the software, and ideally have templates set up – once this is in place the use of word processing software would be beneficial.   2 marks

Spreadsheet software could be used to keep a note of the expenses for the meeting, e.g. catering, travel expenses, venue booking and accommodation, if people needed an overnight stop. The advantage of spreadsheets is that calculating the cost of the meeting and comparing it with the budget is quick and easy. In addition, formulas can be used to help ensure that calculations are performed accurately when the data is entered, thus cutting down on human error.   2 marks

Email software could be used to send out the notice, agenda and minutes of the previous meeting. (These could be sent as attachments.) Email is quicker than normal mail, and it would also help keep printing/copying and distribution costs down. On the other hand, if the internet connection fails, it may mean that some people do not receive the communication – so an alternative way of following up would be worthwhile. In addition, it may be necessary to print some copies for the meeting in case people forget to bring their copies with them.   2 marks

E-diary software could be used to check if people are available for a meeting. This could help avoid a meeting being arranged for a time that many of the attendees have other commitments. It may also be possible to send a meeting request to attendees so that when they accept it the meeting is added to their diary/calendar automatically. This facility will also make it easier for attendees to update their diary if the meeting is changed for some reason. However, it should be noted that a possible problem with using e-diary is that although most people use email as their main communication method, fewer people make proper use of e-diaries. 2 marks

Other packages that could be discussed include databases and the internet.

Question type 2

An administrative assistant will use a variety of software when planning a meeting.

Describe the implications of not using spreadsheet and email software to help with this task.   4 marks

 If spreadsheet software is not used, the implications are that calculations, e.g. in budgets associated with the meeting, would take longer to prepare. [1 mark] They may not follow a house-style, resulting in an inconsistent layout and an increase in errors and confusion.   [1 mark]

If email software is not used, the implications are that documents associated with the meeting would have to be printed and distributed by the normal mail and this would be relatively expensive. [1 mark] The notice of the meeting and agenda would need to be sent out earlier, which could lead to some items for discussion being missed off the agenda.   [1 mark]

2 Unit Assessments (NABs)

Introduction

Administrative Services NAB

Information Technology for Management NAB

Practice time

Practice NAB

INTRODUCTION

You can access the SQA website (www.sqa.org.uk) and look at the unit specification to find out the content of each of the internal units (or go directly to http://www.sqa.org.uk/sqa/39202.html, which is the Higher Administration page).

To locate for the Higher Administration units from the SQA home page, select the **Qualification** tab at the top of the page.

Then choose **National Qualifications**. Scroll down through the **In this Section** box on the left until you see **NQ Unit Search**. Then click this option.

Enter the name of the unit you are searching for e.g. Administrative Services or Information Technology for Management and click **Search**.

Scroll down and open the pdf file that you want – click on it.

Part of your course involves internal assessment. This is when you will sit an end of unit test. NAB stands for National Assessment Bank, which is the place where assessments for all units are deposited with the SQA. Both internal assessments in this course have time limits. The Administrative Services assessment must be completed within 1 hour under exam conditions. The Information Technology for Management Part 1 theory questions must be completed in 30 minutes under exam conditions. The practical Part 2 must be completed in 2 hours and 30 minutes. You can use paper IT manuals and online help during this assessment.

You must pass *all* of the internal assessments. Even if you pass the final exam, you will not gain a Higher in Administration unless you have successfully completed all the NABs.

ADMINISTRATIVE SERVICES NAB

The unit assessments only test the areas covered in that particular unit. The Administrative Services assessment is a series of restricted response questions covering each of the five outcomes. The questions in this particular assessment cover **every outcome** and everything included in those outcomes. In other words, you need to have studied and be sure of all the relevant points before sitting this assessment. See *Higher Administration Course Notes* pages 11–68 for revision.

The questions in Paper 1 of the final exam are more structured than those in the NAB. They demand more in-depth answers which demonstrate a greater overall knowledge of Administration.

The Administrative Services NAB is set out with questions for each outcome. Each NAB is worth approximately 55–60 marks. This means that you can gain a mark per minute of the assessment. You will need 60% of the available marks to pass. The mark allocation for each NAB question tends to be less than those for the questions in Paper 1 of the final exam. This means that you are required to answer the questions by giving the main points. Remember, however, to write in sentences: don't use bullet points in your answer. The questions in the NAB are straightforward – remember, it is a test to check your understanding of what you have learned in that unit and how you can apply that knowledge.

Doing your first NAB is always quite stressful. Being timed is also a worry. You need to make sure that you don't run out of time and lose valuable marks. Time management is very important and, as stated previously, a good guide is to try to write a point a minute. Teachers will usually help you prepare for this test by giving you timed exercises as practice. A good point to remember is not to spend too long puzzling over one question because:

a) you may not get any more marks;

b) you may run out of time and fail to complete the paper.

If you don't know the answer to a question, move on to the next one and get marks for what you do know. You may be able to go back at the end if you have time left.

> Never aim to just pass the NAB: the more marks you can get the better. It is a good test in helping you prepare for the final exam.

NABs alone cannot be used for appeals. However, if you have consistently produced high-scoring work in class, they can be part of the evidence to support an appeal, along with your prelim paper and other tests (such as a second prelim) you may have completed.

INFORMATION TECHNOLOGY FOR MANAGEMENT NAB

There are two parts to the ITFM internal assessment.

Part 1 is a series of short response questions, assessing your knowledge of:

- the role of information in decision making;
- the impact of ICT on workflow, working practices and management and security of information.

This part of the assessment is carried out under controlled, closed book conditions, with a time limit of 30 minutes.

Part 2 is a practical assignment where you will be given a business problem to solve.

The assignment will include activities using:

- email
- e-diary
- presentation software
- the internet
- spreadsheets
- word processing
- databases

The assignment will be carried out under controlled conditions, but you will be allowed to use the online help or paper-based IT manuals if necessary.

This part of the assessment must be completed in 2 hours and 30 minutes.

You must pass both Part 1 and Part 2 of the internal assessment; the pass mark for each part is 60%.

> Be aware that in Part 2 of the ITFM NAB, you must be able to use an e-diary, email, the internet and presentation software. You will not actually be required to use this software in the final exam, but you may be asked a theory question on these areas.

PRACTICE TIME

Sometimes the best way to learn is by doing! Just reading over notes can often be boring and it can be difficult to retain the information.

Why not try a mock Administrative Services NAB in you own time? This is usually the best way of finding out what you don't know and what you need to spend some time revising.

Step 1

Make sure you are familiar with the content of all of the following outcomes in the unit and understand what they mean.

1	Explain strategies which can be employed to ensure effectiveness in the workplace.
2	Describe the impact of changing working practices on the modern working environment.
3	Describe the procedures and processes involved in recruiting, developing and supporting staff.
4	Explain how formal meetings are planned, conducted and supported.
5	Explain the importance of providing effective customer service.

Step 2

Now get yourself ready.

1. Revise your notes.
2. Put aside an hour when you will not be disturbed.
3. Set the timer on your phone.
4. Settle down and answer the questions. Don't peek at your notes – try all the questions and only when finished look at the sample answers pages 27–34.

Administrative Services: closed book (1 hour)

Outcome 1

1. Describe two key differences between the role of a senior and a junior administrator.   2 marks

2. Describe two different methods used by an employee to help with time management.   2 marks

3. Explain the meaning of SMART targets.   2 marks

4. Describe two effects on an employee of poor time management.   2 marks

5. Explain the importance of delegation.   2 marks

6. Describe two features of an effective team.   2 marks

                                                          12 marks

Outcome 2

1. Outline one advantage and one disadvantage of the following work practices:

   (a) flexi-time   2 marks

   (b) career break.   2 marks

2. Describe two disadvantages to an employee of working in an open-plan office.   2 marks

3. Explain the purpose of the Health and Safety Executive.   2 marks

4. Outline the best method of informing new employees of company policies and procedures.   2 marks

5. Being dismissed for breaching organisational policies is one form of disciplinary procedure. State two other forms of procedure that an employer may use.   2 marks

6. Outline any action an employee can take if they have been dismissed.   2 marks

14 marks

Outcome 3

1. Outline an advantage and a disadvantage of:

   (a) internal recruitment   2 marks

   (b) external recruitment.   2 marks

2. Describe a circumstance when an employee may choose external staff training as opposed to internal staff training.   2 marks

3. Give two advantages of in-house training.   2 marks

4. Describe the main purpose of a staff appraisal scheme.   2 marks

5. Describe two benefits to the employer of having a staff welfare policy.   2 marks

12 marks

Outcome 4

1. Compare and contrast an AGM with a committee meeting.   4 marks

2. Describe two responsibilities that need to be performed after the meeting by:

   (*a*) the secretary   2 marks

   (*b*) the chairperson.   2 marks

3. Explain two of the following terms used in the conduct of meetings:

   (*a*) ballot

   (*b*) adjournment

   (*c*) verbatim

   (*d*) motion.   2 marks

4. Describe how electronic diaries have had an impact on the organisation and conduct of meetings.   2 marks

   12 marks

Outcome 5

1. Explain the purpose of a customer care strategy.   2 marks

2. Poor customer service may result in complaints. Describe two different methods an organisation can use in dealing with complaints.   2 marks

3. Being customer focused helps improve effective customer service. Explain how an organisation can be customer focused.   2 marks

   6 marks

   TOTAL 56 marks

Administrative Services: suggested answers

It is sometimes a good idea to repeat the question in your answer to help focus your thoughts, but keep an eye on your time. Always look at the mark allocation. If there are 2 marks allocated, you must give two clear points. See where the ✓ appears in the suggested answer, as this indicates a possible mark.

Write in sentences – one-word answers or bulleted lists will not gain many marks.

Outcome 1

> **1.** Describe two key differences between the role of a senior
>   and a junior administrator.   **2 marks**

 A senior administrator will supervise and delegate work that needs to be done, possibly issuing deadlines.✓ A junior will follow procedures, complete given tasks and work as a member of a team.✓

In order to make clear the distinction here you would need to give examples of what each employee does.

> **2.** Describe two different methods used by an employee to
>   help with time management.   **2 marks**

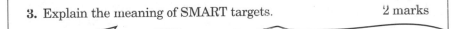 A to-do list is usually a note to yourself giving a list of tasks that need to be done in an order of priority. The tasks are crossed off the list as they are completed.✓

An e-diary is useful for keeping appointments and sending reminders, and can be accessed from any PC or laptop with internet access.✓

(Other answers could have included: wall planner, Gantt chart or action plan.)
In a 'describe' question you must do more than just mention the method.

> **3.** Explain the meaning of SMART targets.   **2 marks**

 In order to set a target that can be met it should be:

S = specific, for example, 30 new records must be keyed into the database.

M = measureable, for example, there are 30 records.

A = achievable, for example, there is one hour in which to do this task.

R = realistic, for example, the office junior is familiar with databases and is familiar with this type of work.

T = time-bound, for example, the task needs to be completed by lunchtime today.

As this is an 'explain' question you are expected to expand on the meanings.

---

4. Describe two effects on an employee of poor time management.   2 marks

---

 Low morale ✔ because they are not getting things completed. Increased stress ✔ as work commitments start to pile up.

By developing the effect you are fulfilling the 'describe' command.

---

5. Explain the importance of delegation.   2 marks

 It helps to develop staff, improves motivation,✔ saves time and leaves the manager free for more important work.✔

---

6. Describe two features of an effective team.   2 marks

Two features of an effective team are:
individuals within the team taking responsibility for set tasks ✔ and suggesting ideas and being prepared to reach compromises. ✔

12 marks

Outcome 2

---

1. Outline one advantage and one disadvantage of the following work practices:

(*a*) flexi-time   2 marks

 An advantage would be the opportunity to plan personal time for things like appointments and dealing with family matters. ✔

A disadvantage would be that it can sometimes be difficult to find time to take accrued leave. ✔

With this type of question make sure that you don't just 'flip' the disadvantage. Always make a clear distinction between what is an advantage and what is a disadvantage.

(*b*) career break   2 marks

An advantage would be to allow the opportunity of improved work/life balance and maybe take the opportunity to do something completely different, like working overseas. ✓

A disadvantage may be that time away from work could result in the need for some retraining. ✓

---

2. Describe two disadvantages to an employee of working in an open-plan office.   2 marks

Lack of privacy ✓ due to no personal space.

Unable to control the environment, ✓ for instance the temperature, ventilation or light, to suit personal preferences.

Note how the answer is always developed – that little bit of further explanation will get the mark.

---

3. Explain the purpose of the Health and Safety Executive.   2 marks

If an organisation has not followed health and safety guidelines then the HSE can inspect the premises and enforce the law. ✓ If required, they can fine the organisation or even close it down. ✓

---

4. Outline the best method of informing new employees of company policies and procedures.   2 marks

Induction ✓ – as at this point they will receive information, training and copies of policies and procedures. ✓

5. Being dismissed for breaching organisational policies is one form of disciplinary procedure. State two other forms of procedure that an employer may use.   **2 marks**

 They could suspend the employee with or without pay.✔ They could fine them by taking money from their wages.✔

6. Outline any action an employee can take if they have been dismissed.   **2 marks**

 They can appeal the decision ✔ and their case may be heard by a special tribunal where they can put their side of the case to an independent body.✔

14 marks

Outcome 3

1. Outline an advantage and a disadvantage of:

(*a*) internal recruitment   **2 marks**

 An advantage of internal recruitment is that the employee is already known to the firm.✔

A disadvantage of internal recruitment is that it may be difficult to find the right replacement for the vacancy.✔

In an 'outline' question you don't have to give the 'because' or 'why' bit of the answer – it is more of a statement.

(*b*) external recruitment   **2 marks**

An advantage of external recruitment is that it introduces fresh ideas and skills.✔

A disadvantage of external recruitment is that the recruitment process may be more expensive and it may take longer.✔

2. Describe a circumstance when an employee may choose external staff training as opposed to internal staff training.   2 marks

If the employee wishes to gain recognised certification ✓ for the training, for example an SQA qualification, then they may need to choose external training by attending a college. ✓

3. Give two advantages of in-house training.   2 marks

It can be tailored to suit specific needs.✓ Employees will not need to travel ✓ to the training if it is held in-house.

4. Describe the main purpose of a staff appraisal scheme.   2 marks

The main purpose is to help to identify staff development and training requirements ✓ and to allow two-way feedback between employee and manager on work role and responsibilities.✓

5. Describe two benefits to the employer of having a staff welfare policy.   2 marks

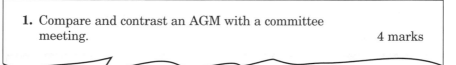
Benefits of a staff welfare policy include more motivated staff,✓ better working conditions and information available to staff.✓   **12 marks**

Outcome 4

1. Compare and contrast an AGM with a committee meeting.   4 marks

This type of question is always seen as one of the most difficult questions to answer. Try to make sure you use words like 'whereas' and 'on the other hand' in your answer.

 An AGM is held once a year.✔ It is used to discuss the company's performance and to elect new office bearers ✔ whereas the committee meeting is usually held to discuss a certain type of business, ✔ such as advisory, executive or ad hoc business. It may take place on a more regular basis, ✔ for example, weekly or monthly.

---

2. Describe two responsibilities that need to be performed after the meeting by:

(*a*) the secretary   2 marks

 The secretary will tidy up the room and alert reception that the meeting is finished.✔

The secretary will prepare the minutes of the meeting with the chairperson.✔

(*b*) the chairperson   2 marks

 The chairperson will follow up discussions and action point with members of the meeting.✔

The chairperson will liaise with the secretary over the minutes and the next agenda.✔

---

3. Explain two of the following terms used in the conduct of meetings:

(*a*) ballot   2 marks

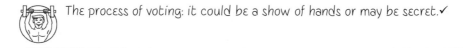 The process of voting: it could be a show of hands or may be secret.✔

(*b*) adjournment

When a meeting is stopped because, for example, they have run out of time or further research needs to be undertaken before discussion can continue, but will be resumed at a later date.✓

(c) verbatim

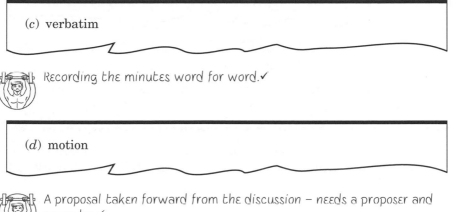 Recording the minutes word for word.✓

(d) motion

A proposal taken forward from the discussion – needs a proposer and seconder.✓

4. Describe how electronic diaries have had an impact on the organisation and conduct of meetings.   2 marks

 Invitations can be sent to attendees of a meeting and it will automatically be recorded in their diaries.✓ Reminders can be sent on the previous day or even 15 minutes beforehand to ensure members attend.✓

With a question like this be careful you don't just describe an electronic diary – it's the **impact** they have had on the organisation of a meeting that needs to be described.   **12 marks**

Outcome 5

1. Explain the purpose of a customer care strategy.   2 marks

 This is a statement about the standards ✓ that a customer can expect from an organisation with regards to its product(s) and the service that can be expected.✓

2. Poor customer service may result in complaints. Describe two different methods an organisation can use in dealing with complaints.   2 marks

Complaints can be dealt with by specially trained staff who know how to follow the correct procedures.✓

Complaints can be logged when received and dealt with within a set time frame.✓

3. Being customer focused helps improve effective customer service. Explain how an organisation can be customer focused.   2 marks

By ensuring that they listen to their customers' requirements.✓ By providing guarantees and warranties, and providing special staff training.✓   6 marks

TOTAL 56 marks

Right, how many marks did you gain? Remember, you need 60% to pass, so you would need to get at least 34 out of 56 in the previous exercise. Make sure you note where you went wrong and revise those topic areas again.

It is now time to look at the ITFM NAB. It comes in two parts. We will start with Part 1. This is a bit like Administrative Services in that it is a series of short questions assessing your knowledge in the areas of:

● the role of information in decision making;

● the impact of ICT on workflow, working practices and management and security of information.

This part of the NAB is out of approximately 26–28 marks and again you need to get 60% to pass.

Before starting, revise pages 69–95 in *Higher Administration Course Notes*.

Now get yourself ready.

1. Revise your notes.

2. Put aside 30 minutes when you will not be disturbed.

3. Set the timer on your phone.

4. Answer the questions. Don't peek at your notes – try all the questions and only when finished look at the sample answers on pages 36–39.

Information Technology for Management Part 1 (outcomes 1 and 2): closed book (30 minutes)

Outcome 1

1. Outline two different sources of information. Describe how each source can be used, giving an example. **4 marks**

2. Quantitative and qualitative information may be presented in a number of ways. For both of these terms identify the type of information you would be working with, and which software would be used to present it. **2 marks**

3. Information for decision making needs to be meaningful. Describe two other features of such information. **2 marks**

4. Identify two different levels of management. Give an example of the type of decision that each level may make with regard to ICT. **4 marks**

12 marks

Outcome 2

1. Describe one effect that ICT has had on workflow at the input, processing and output stages. **3 marks**

2. Describe how ICT has allowed more people to work from home. **2 marks**

3. Electronic file management is part of the data management process. Explain how electronic file management can improve efficiency of data management. **2 marks**

4. Losing customers could be a consequence of poor data management. Outline two examples of poor data management. **2 marks**

5. Describe three ways of ensuring the security and confidentiality of paper-based information. **3 marks**

6. Identify the legislation and give an example of how an organisation might infringe copyright law. **2 marks**

14 marks

TOTAL 26 marks

Information Technology for Management Part 1: suggested answers

The same principle we used in Administrative Services applies here. Always look at the mark allocation: if 2 marks are allocated, you must give two clear points. See where the ✓ appears in the suggested answer, as this indicates a possible point.

Write in sentences – one-word answers or bulleted lists will not gain many marks.

Outcome 1

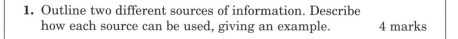

> **1.** Outline two different sources of information. Describe how each source can be used, giving an example.   4 marks

 Primary – this is first-hand information, often collected face-to-face.✓ It will be used when information is required for a specific purpose and collected in one-to-one interviews or by using questionnaires.✓

Secondary – this is second-hand information that has already been collected, such as government statistics ✓ It will have been gathered for one purpose but can be reused for another purpose.✓

To get all the marks for this question, you need to make sure you definitely say when each source would be used and give an example. This answer has given the questionnaire as an example of primary information and government statistics as secondary.

> **2.** Quantitative and qualitative information may be presented in a number of ways. For both of these terms identify the type of information you would be working with, and which software would be used to present it.   2 marks

 Quantitative information is usually measuring something like sales figures and would therefore be best presented in graphs, charts or worksheets using spreadsheet software.✓

Qualitative information is more descriptive, like a report, and therefore lends itself to written presentation, so presentation software (e. g. PowerPoint or word processing software) would be best used to present it.✓

3. Information for decision making needs to be meaningful.
Describe two other features of such information. 2 marks

Accurate – this means that information needs to be correct and from a reliable source.✓

Up-to-date   this means that information needs to be current.✓

4. Identify two different levels of management. Give an
example of the type of decision that each level may
make with regard to ICT. 4 marks

Strategic Management – make the long-term decisions,✓ for example to change their sales strategy to sell only online.✓

Operational Management – the managers who make the day-to-day decisions ✓ regarding the running of the organisation. An operational decision may be to adopt a standard company email signature.✓

If you are given the choice, it is always best to choose strategic and operational management, because there is a much clearer definition between these two levels of management than others. Tactical management is more difficult to explain.

12 marks

Outcome 2

1. Describe one effect that ICT has had on workflow at
the input, processing and output stages. 3 marks

At the input stage, email has allowed for information to be sent, collated and replied to much more quickly than before.✓

At the processing stage, software like spreadsheets, databases and word processing has allowed the information collected to be analysed much more easily.✓

At the output stage, information analysed can now be presented in easily read formats such as reports, presentations and graphs.✓

2. Describe how ICT has allowed more people to work from home. **2 marks**

Email for communicating, mobile phones for contact, video-conferencing for meetings and e-diaries and intranets for recording information ✓ all mean there is no longer a need for anyone to be based in an office at all times. With the right pieces of equipment and software people can communicate ✓ with others in different parts of the country or world.

Remember that ICT stands for information and communications technology, so make sure you mention both in your answer.

3. Electronic file management is part of the data management process. Explain how electronic file management can improve efficiency of data management. **2 marks**

Electronic file management is making sure that there are proper procedures for naming, storage, archiving and deletion of files. ✓ If these are done properly, data will be found quickly and efficiently. ✓

4. Losing customers could be a consequence of poor data management. Outline two examples of poor data management. **2 marks**

Allowing everyone access to all files – this could result in security breaches. ✓

Not keeping information and records up to date – this could result in bad decisions. ✓

5. Describe three ways of ensuring the security and confidentiality of paper-based information. **3 marks**

Keep all personal and confidential files in locked cabinets and ensure that keys are kept in safe places.

Restrict access to visitors to certain areas of the organisation; this can be done by making sure they have badges or by using technology, for example, palm or eye scanners. ✓

Dispose of any papers by shredding or other appropriate means, for example, special confidential uplift sacks. ✓

---

6. Identify the legislation and give an example of how an organisation might infringe copyright law.   **2 marks**

 The legislation is the Copyright, Design and Patents Act 1988. ✓

An organisation which copies materials from textbooks or journals may be breaking the above act. ✓

14 marks

TOTAL 26 marks

How did you get on? You need to get 16 marks to pass this section. Go back and revise anything that caused you problems or ask your teacher for help.

Information Technology for Management: practical

This next section gives guidance on how to deal with the e diary, internet, presentations and email tasks in the practical paper. Remember, these tasks are ONLY assessed in the NAB and are not in paper 2 of the practical exam. However, you could be asked a theory question on features and functions of these applications.

See Chapter 3 for guidance on word processing, spreadsheets and databases.

Electronic diary (e-diary)

No new content is introduced at Higher level, but you must be able to use all of the features introduced at earlier levels. Tick off the ones that you are able to do – and revise your notes or ask your teacher about any you are unsure of.

	✓
schedule appointment	
set reminder	
print calendar: daily, weekly, monthly views	
schedule meeting	
schedule recurrent meetings	
navigate the calendar, for example, find appointments, dates or notes	

The e-diary task will most probably ask you to arrange a meeting.

Please arrange a 2 hour meeting for me with the branch managers from Aberdeen, Dundee and Perth some time during July (in my office). As some people will be travelling a fair distance, a lunchtime meeting would be good, e.g. 12.00–2.00p.m. (We could have a buffet lunch.)

Availability

Me	Available any time after the 5th
Amy Borthwick (Aberdeen)	Can't make the 4th, 15th or 29th
Jack Wilson (Dundee)	Goes on holiday on the 26th
Dave Duncan (Perth)	On holiday 30th June to 12th July inclusive

Select a suitable date

I would like you to accompany me, so make an entry in your own e-diary.

Print a copy of your e-dairy in weekly view showing the meeting details.

Thanks, Joe

To complete the task you need to:

- work out a suitable date and time;
- enter it into your e-diary;
- print the correct details from your e-diary in weekly view.

To help you work out a suitable date, highlight the key points in the message.

> Please arrange a 2 hour meeting for me with the branch managers from Aberdeen, Dundee and Perth some time during July (in my office). As some people will be travelling a fair distance, a lunchtime meeting would be good, e.g. 12.00–2.00p.m. (We could have a buffet lunch.)
>
> **Availability**
>
> | | |
> |---|---|
> | Me | Available any time after the 5th |
> | Amy Borthwick (Aberdeen) | Can't make the 4th, 15th or 29th |
> | Jack Wilson (Dundee) | Goes on holiday on the 26th |
> | Dave Duncan (Perth) | On holiday 30th June to 12th July inclusive |
>
> **Select a suitable date**
>
> I would like you to accompany me, so make an entry in your own e-diary.
>
> Print a copy of your e-dairy in weekly view showing the meeting details.
>
> Thanks, Joe

- Dave Duncan can't do anything until 13 July (and would probably prefer not to have a meeting that involved travelling on his first day back).

- Jack Wilson can't do anything from 27 July (and would probably prefer not to have a meeting on 26 July if he goes on holiday that day).

So that narrows it down to 14–25 July. Within these dates, everyone is available except Amy, who can't do 15 July – so any day 14–25 July *except* 15 July would be good. The time suggested was 12.00–2.00p.m. – so go with this when you enter the details in your e-diary.

Give your meeting a suitable subject, such as 'branch managers' meeting', and don't forget the venue (Joe's office).

19 July	22 July	
20 July	**23 July**	
12:00 – 14:00 Branch managers' meeting (Joe's office)		
21 July	**24 July**	**25 July**

You would normally get 3 marks for this task.

Task	Marks
Select suitable date for meeting	1
Enter details correctly into diary	1
Print e-diary page as instructed	1
Total	**3**

You may also have a venue to consider.

AUTUMN CONFERENCE PLANNING

I would like you to arrange a meeting for me to get together with the team leaders to discuss the autumn conference arrangements – some time during the last full working week in June. All team leaders must attend. We will need to use meeting room 1. The meeting will last 1 hour.

Availability:
Peter is taking Friday off.
Gill is out on Wednesday afternoon.

Meeting room 1 is not available on Monday afternoon or Wednesday afternoon.

I would like you to attend too, so please enter the appointment in your e-diary.
Print a copy of your e-diary in weekly view, showing the appointment you have made.

Again, highlight the important bits

AUTUMN CONFERENCE PLANNING

I would like you to arrange a meeting for me to get together with the team leaders to discuss the autumn conference arrangements – some time during the last full working week in June. All team leaders must attend. We will need to use meeting room 1. The meeting will last 1 hour.

Availability:
Peter is taking Friday off.
Gill is out on Wednesday afternoon.

Meeting room 1 is not available on Monday afternoon or Wednesday afternoon.

I would like you to attend too, so please enter the appointment in your e-diary.
Print a copy of your e-diary in weekly view, showing the appointment you have made.

- This meeting should take place during the last full working week in June. (If you are doing this task in 2010 that would be the week commencing 21 June.)
- Person availability – can't do Friday (at all) or Wednesday afternoon.
- Room availability – can't do Monday afternoon or Wednesday afternoon.
- So you have Monday morning, Tuesday, Wednesday morning and Thursday to choose from.

Other things to consider

Give your meeting a suitable name, such as *Autumn conference planning meeting* and remember to state the venue – *Meeting room 1*.

21 June	24 June	
	10:00–11:00 Autumn conference planning meeting (Meeting room 1)	
22 June	25 June	
23 June	26 June	27 June

Internet

This is the part that you would imagine being the easy bit – but you still need to take care.

Any of the following internet skills could be assessed in the NAB. Tick off the ones you are sure of – if you are unsure of any, go back to your notes or speak to your teacher.

	✓
Open browser	
Use search engines	
Open website	
Navigate hyperlinks	
Copy information from web page to word processing document	
Use history feature	
Use favourites and bookmarks	
Print information	
Integrate information from the internet into a word processing document	
Insert hyperlink to URL in a word processing or presentation file	
Customise searches	
Understand the use of cookies	

If you are asked to locate a relevant website on the internet, make sure that the site you find is indeed appropriate to the task you are doing.

If you are asked to insert a hyperlink to a web page (for instance in a presentation file or word processed document) make sure that your hyperlink works, and that it takes you to the website you intended.

A task in your NAB might read something like this:

> Search the internet for information on holidays in Scotland.
>
> Insert a relevant URL after 'More information can be found at ...' on slide 3. Create a hyperlink to the site.

Or you may be given a URL and asked to enter it into your file, then create a hyperlink from it to the site.

So the task would be more like this:

> Insert a hyperlink to http://www.leckieandleckie.co.uk/ on the slide with the title 'Support Materials'.

If you are asked to search for a relevant URL use any search engine you like – Google is popular.

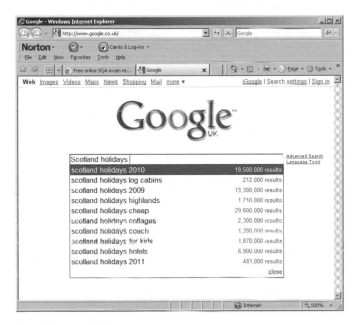

Marks could be allocated like this:

Task	Marks
Select appropriate website (if asked to search for one)	1
URL added to correct slide/location	1
URL hyperlinks to correct website	1
Total	**3**

Some searches will return many possible sites.

Be more specific to reduce the number of sites returned

If you can't find something that looks appropriate in the first page or two, try being more specific in your search.

Tips to help you search more efficiently

- If you are looking for a phrase surround it with quotation marks, e.g. **"Edinburgh Castle"**.

- If you want to exclude a word from your search, put a minus (–) in front of the word, e.g. –Dundee.

- If you want local sites, just search pages from the UK rather than the whole web.

Miss out pages that mention the highlands or golf

Search the whole web or just pages from the UK?

If you are searching for a phrase put it in quotation marks.

If you are asked to find a site, take a quick look at it to check that it is suitable – but don't get distracted and spend too much time on it (a dangerous time-stealer in a timed assessment)!

You will often find that if you copy a URL from the address bar and paste it into your slide/document the hyperlink from the URL will be created automatically.

Presentations

Make sure you can perform all of the following. Tick the relevant box when you can. If you are unsure go back to your class notes or see your teacher.

	✓
Insert text using two fonts	
Use bold, italics, underscore, centring	
Delete and edit text	
Insert and delete a graphic	

47

Add text to a graphic	
Use bullets	
Create chart, table, organisation chart within presentation software	
Add and delete a slide	
Animate text/objects	
Import data from a word processed document	
Find and replace text	
Change line spacing and font size	
Align, distribute and group objects	
Change slide content layout	
Apply slide transitions	
Import data or chart from spreadsheet	
Change slide order (move and copy slides)	
View slides	
Use slide master to:	
• apply and change background	
• apply and change colour scheme	
• apply and change design templates	
• define and redefine fonts and styles	
• insert footer objects	
• insert action buttons	
• customise bullets and numbers	
Print presentation in slide and handout formats	
Advance slides automatically, timed to accommodate speaker notes	
Promote and demote text within slides	
Import data from the internet	
Hyperlink to URL	
Create and print notes	

Remember – in the final exam you could be asked to explain any of the above presentation features in a theory question.

In this task you will normally be given 4–6 slides to update.

Winter Sports

Fun for everyone

Competition sports
- Skiing
- Snowboarding
- Bobsleigh
- Snowmobiling
- Ice skating
- Curling
- Biathlon
- Ice hockey

Just for fun
- Sledging
- Building snowmen
- Snowball fights
- Sliding

Where to go...
- Highlands
- Swiss Alps
- French Alps
- Whistler
- Lapland

Major sporting events
- Winter Olympics
- Winter Paralympics
- Asian Winter Games

When you open the presentation file, take a few minutes to have a look at it so that you know what you are dealing with.

The presentation task would be similar to this:

> Open the presentation file which has been emailed to you and update it as follows:
>
> 1. Insert a suitable background on all slides.
>
> 2. Add page numbering to the footer of all slides except the title slide.
>
> 3. Use the internet to find out what 'biathlon' is in relation to winter sports and add a note to the 'Competition sports' slide so that I can tell people what it is.
>
> 4. Add a master title slide and add the logo to it – put it to the left of the title/subtitle. Add the logo to the slide master so that it appears on the top right corner of all slides except the title slide. Resize the logos as necessary to get a good effect.
>
> 5. The slides 'Competition sports' and 'Where to go ...' – change the layout so that the bullets and pictures change sides. Resize the graphics if necessary.
>
> 6. Add a text box to the end of the last slide that says 'Prepared by [*your name*]'.
>
> 7. Set all slides to advance automatically after 1 minute.
>
> 8. Print the presentation – six slides to the page (handout format).

Read the instructions carefully when carrying out this task and try not to miss anything out.

Be careful with PowerPoint – it is easy to get distracted checking out all the different effects and colour and formatting options. Don't get caught up with 'don't like that ... try something else ...'. You will just end up wasting time. Anything that does what the task asks will be acceptable – even if you think you could find something better if you had time.

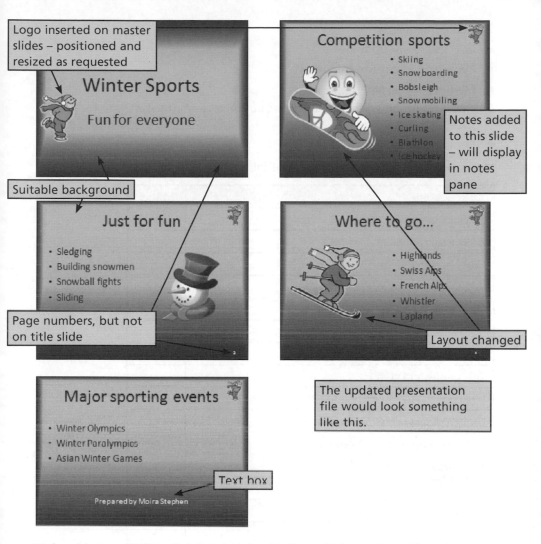

To be able to complete the above task using PowerPoint you would need to use the following features:

- Format background
- View header & footer
- Search on the internet – and add a suitable note to the slide
- View the slide master

- Add a title master
- Insert a picture from file
- Reposition and resize the picture
- Change slide layout
- Add a transition effect that advances automatically after 1 minute for all slides
- Print the presentation

Marks would probably be allocated like this:

Task	Marks
Suitable background added	1
Background added to all slides	1
Slides numbered	1
Slide number in correct position	1
Slide number not on title slide	1
Note added to correct slide	1
Note contains information requested	1
Title master added	1
Logo positioned correctly on title master	1
Logo positioned correctly on slide master	1
Logo resized/moved as necessary	1
Slide layout changed	1
Slides advance automatically	1
Slides advance at 1 minute intervals	1
Text box added to last slide	1
Information in text box correct	1
Print in handout format	1
Total	**17**

Email

Your email task will ask you to send your presentation (as an attachment) to your teacher/lecturer.

You could be asked to do any of the following to complete the task – tick off the ones that you are sure of in the lists here (and check out any you are unsure of).

	✓		✓
Read mail		Compose and enter text	
Use reply feature		Send mail	
Use address book		Print email	
Use cc		Use bcc	
Mark urgent		Create attachment/s	
Create contact group		Create signature	
Find an email		Create folders	
Automatically manage messages		Archive old messages	
Create automated responses		Be aware of email etiquette	

The last bit of this task usually says something like:

Email the presentation back to your tutor marked urgent (or high priority).

With this task, be careful that you remember to do everything that is asked.

Correct email address

Appropriate subject

Correct file attached

Marked high priority

Make sure the body of the email is formal and business-like and has no typing or spelling errors.

DON'T just type *"here it is"*.

Marks would probably be allocated like this:

Task	Marks
Open email with attachment (if presentation emailed to you)	1
Send email with attachment	2
Mark email urgent	1
Total	**4**

PRACTICE NAB

When you are ready, you can try practice practical NAB which includes word processing, spreadsheet and database exercises (and a suggested solution) on Leckie & Leckie's website at:

http://www.leckieandleckie.co.uk/products/buy_online.asp?css=1&area=202&lvl=4&id=2066

3 The Final Examination

Introduction

Tackling Section 1

Tackling Section 2

Paper 2

Spreadsheets

Databases

Word processing

Conclusion

INTRODUCTION

As stated in the Introduction (page 6), there are two papers for the final examination in Administration. Paper 1 is the theory paper and Paper 2 is the practical paper. Both papers last for 1 hour and 20 minutes and there is a break of 20 minutes between papers. You have to work hard in this subject because not only do you have to show your knowledge and understanding, you also have to demonstrate your practical skills under timed conditions.

Let's take a closer look at Paper 1.

This paper is in two sections. Section 1 is based on a short case-study with questions. There is no choice in this section – you must complete all of the questions. Section 1 is worth 20 marks. The questions in this section reflect the theme of the case-study.

Some candidates prefer to start with Section 2, where they can choose to write about topics with which they are more familiar. This is not a problem – you can tackle the paper any way you want. However, you do have to watch your time and make sure that you clearly label which questions you are answering.

From exam diet 2010 onwards, 'compare' questions will now ONLY appear in section 1 of the paper.

Section 2 consists of five extended response questions, from which you must choose two. Each question is worth 20 marks.

'It was disappointing to read from markers that there were increasing numbers of candidates whose handwriting was extremely difficult to read.'

SQA External Assessment Report

This is not an English exam, but it is still important to write in sentences and to lay your work out neatly. You should number each answer accurately and leave a clear line between each answer to make it obvious where one answer ends and the next one starts. You should avoid using bullet point answers because this immediately gives a bad impression, though it is a good idea to use short sentences to avoid straying from the point.

'Candidates are still not developing the describe questions, expanding or giving examples in their answers.'

SQA External Assessment Report

At Higher level there is a greater expectation that you should write a 'proper answer' as this will show the depth of your knowledge and understanding. There are a few basic rules which help:

● Try to avoid simple spelling mistakes.

● Write in sentences.

● Keep to the point and don't make up what you don't know.

● Always refer back to the question to keep on track.

Your teacher will have told you that you must 'develop' your answer. You can see from the SQA report that it is a fairly common mistake for candidates not to do this. But what exactly does 'develop' mean?

In Chapter 1, pages 8–17, we looked closely at the command words. The ones that usually require some development in the answer are **describe**, **discuss** and **compare**.

To gain marks in a 'describe' question you first need to outline what you are talking about, then give an example. In other words, you need to give two points to get 1 mark.

In a 'discuss' question you would be expected to make a number of points equal to the number of marks being given for the question. If the marker thinks you have just described and not actually made a discussion then you will only be given half the marks, even if what you have said is correct.

The 'compare' question is probably the most difficult. This is because you need to make a complete statement of comparison to get 1 mark, though you can compare similarities. In the 2010 exam the compare question will be in Section A, which makes it compulsory – so you will have to know how to answer it.

Developing your answer means giving more information than just a statement. It is your chance to show the examiner how much you know. Just be careful that you answer according to the command word. To make your answers read well you can use some linking words or phrases to add additional information as shown below.

Describe	for example
When giving the example you could say:	such as
	can be seen as
Discuss	the fact that
A discussion means that, in a way, you argue with yourself as you put forward different points using:	it can be considered
	accordingly
	consequently
	it would seem that
Compare	whereas
Give two sides of the story with words such as:	similarly
	in comparison to
	equally
	likewise
	on the other hand

TACKLING SECTION 1

Let's consider the 2009 Paper 1. On the front cover there is guidance to help you with your time management. It is suggested that Section 1 should take approximately 30 minutes and Section 2 about 50 minutes.

Take time to read the case-study first. You may find it useful to highlight or underline key words and phrases in it. The case-study will not give you the answers to any of the questions but it is designed to start you thinking on the right lines. You have to attempt **all** the questions in Section 1. In 2009 the case-study was on the induction and training of staff at McDonalds' restaurants. In general, the first question is very straightforward, so that you get into the paper and build up your confidence – it will often use one of the easier command words, such as 'outline'.

In 2009 the two questions that caused candidates the most difficulty were numbers 4 and 5.

> **4.** Describe features of presentation software which may be used to enhance the delivery of a training session.   4 marks

'Candidates found great difficulty in describing the features of presentation software. A number attempted to describe other forms of software and even hardware such as OHPs and data projectors.'

SQA External Assessment Report

So how should this question be answered?

Well, it's a 'describe' question, so you must make sure there is development in the answer. It is worth 4 marks so you will need to make at least two good points. A good answer could be:

One feature is the use of animation, which allows text and graphics to be introduced by movement, such as "flying in" or "spinning". ✓ This allows the presenter to focus on important points. ✓

This software also allows the creation and printing of notes ✓ from the slides which trainees can use for reference. ✓

Other features that could have been used as examples are:

- using different slide layouts
- using sound or video clips
- using hyperlinks to other files/PowerPoints
- the use of master slides
- timing the presentation.

> **5.** Discuss the features of an effective team.   6 marks

This question is worth 6 marks and you will need to discuss the answer. An example of a poor answer could be:

The features of an effective team are that there will be better communication and decision making. The team can share goals and knowledge and will be able to work together on projects which usually allows members to adopt roles that suit them best.

Looking at this answer you could be tempted to say that this candidate has mentioned five reasonable points. However, are the points mentioned features or benefits of team working? There has been no attempt at discussion – remember that you would be expected to use some of the key phrases from the table on page 57.

A better answer would be:

The features of an effective team are that there will be a strong leader who will give advice and monitor the workload, ✓ and consequently the team will help make decisions and take responsibility for set tasks. ✓ They all need to be working towards a shared goal. ✓ In doing this there will be support for each other ✓ and they will be able to bring out each other's strengths and/or weaknesses. ✓ It would seem that teams that do work together are more prepared to compromise, ✓ share work and allow different members with different skills to adopt roles and perform to their strengths. ✓

In the 2008 Paper 1, Section 1, the theme of the case-study was 'leadership, teamworking and getting the best from your staff'.

> The answers to the questions are not in the case-study, but always make sure that you read it carefully as it will give you a good idea of where to base your answers.

The questions that were not well done in 2008 were numbers 3 and 4.

> **3.** Discuss the advantages and disadvantages of recruiting internally and externally.   6 marks

'Although advantages and disadvantages of both internal and external recruitment were discussed, candidates frequently gave the "flip side" of the argument, this gained no further marks.'

SQA External Assessment Report (2008)

So what does this mean? Well, if you are asked to give the advantages and disadvantages of internal and external recruitment, don't say it is cheaper to recruit internally and more expensive to recruit externally. That is just 'flipping' the argument, so gains no extra marks.

You really need to give different advantages and disadvantages, for example:

External recruitment allows the opportunity of introducing fresh ideas and new talent to the organisation, ✓ however, it does mean that the recruitment process will take longer. ✓ Internal recruitment, on the other hand, improves morale and provides development opportunities for staff, ✓ however, it can sometimes result in bad feeling if other staff feel they have been passed over for promotion. ✓ External recruitment increases flexibility, as it is easier to select a better quality of applicant. ✓ On the other hand, this could be more costly, as new staff will require extra training on company procedures and a longer period of induction. ✓

---

4. The job description and person specification are used in the recruitment and selection process. Compare these two documents.

4 marks

'Comparison of the job description and the person specification was very badly done – candidates struggled to give 4 separate statements of comparison.'

SQA External Assessment Report

You will only get one mark for each complete statement. You don't get the mark for just mentioning one of the items being compared. For example, a poor answer to this question would be:

A job description is made up according to the requirements of the job and a person specification is completed after job analysis. ✓ A job description has the duties and responsibilities, whereas the person specification has the essential and desirable qualities of the post. ✓

This answer would only get 2 marks because only two complete statements have been given, though it could be said there are four points in the answer.

A better answer to this question would be:

The job specification and the person specification both result from a job analysis. ✓ *Information from both documents will then be used to put together the job advertisement.* ✓ *In addition, both documents are used by the candidate and the organisation in preparation for the interview.* ✓ *The job description shows the duties and responsibilities expected from the job holder, whereas the person specification details the personal qualities and skills required for the job.* ✓

An important point to note in 'compare' questions is that you don't always have to give a true comparison – you can say what is similar about both items you are discussing, as can be seen in the answer above.

In the 2007 Paper 1, Section 1, question 5 caused candidates some difficulty.

'Some candidates had difficulty distinguishing between consequences and implications even when prompted by the word "long-term". Some candidates thought that implications meant problem solving, and a variety of solutions were given as their answer.'

SQA External Assessment Report

> **5.** Identify two possible consequences of poor data management to an organisation and discuss the long-term implications. 6 marks

This was a difficult question and worth more than 25% of the marks in Section 1 of the paper. You really need to make sure you know the difference between the words 'consequence' and 'implication'.

In order to answer this question you need to do two things:

- identify two consequences – worth 2 marks
- discuss the implications – 4 marks

If you don't attempt to discuss the implications, even giving four correct implications will only gain you 50% of the 4 available marks.

A good answer could be:

Two possible consequences of poor data management are that some information may be out of date, which will mean wasting time searching for the correct information. ✓ *Files or data could be lost due to incorrect file-management procedures.* ✓

The implications of this are that work flow can be disrupted, as people have to search for data ✔ that should be easily accessible, and accordingly this could result in bad decision making if the wrong or incorrect data is used, as well as a reduction in efficiency. ✔ Customers could become dissatisfied if incorrect information on them is kept, and they may then choose to go elsewhere, ✔ leading to loss of business for the organisation. ✔

TACKLING SECTION 2

In this section you only have to do two questions, though there are five to choose from. The five questions cover the whole Higher Administration course, including some theory associated with ICT. The topics, however, are not in any order and you will need to make sure that you read ALL the questions carefully before you decide which ones you are going to answer.

How do you do this effectively, given that you only have approximately 50 minutes to answer both questions? Perhaps putting a tick beside the questions you think you know most about might help – or if you have a highlighter use that – and then identify the questions that have the most ticks/highlights.

SECTION 2   *Marks*

Answer any TWO questions.

1.   (*a*)   Outline **2** features of a Mission Statement and justify the importance of this statement to the organisation. ✔   **4**

      (*b*)   Outline **4** factors to be considered to ensure internal customer satisfaction. ✔   **4**

      (*c*)   Discuss strategies used by senior administrative assistants to improve their efficiency in task management. ✔   **8**

      (*d*)   Identify **2** time stealers and for each suggest how these can be avoided.   **4**

                                                                (20)

2.   (*a*)   Outline the benefits of a career break to: ✔

          (i)   the organisation;

          (ii)   the employee.   **4**

      (*b*)   Discuss ways in which flexible working practices can improve the work/life balance of employees.   **8**

      (*c*)   Describe:

          (i)   **2** methods of voting at meetings;   **4**

          (ii)   **2** documents relating to a formal meeting.   **4**

                                                                (20)

---

3. (*a*) Outline ways in which an organisation can:

  (i) monitor e-mail;

  (ii) limit access to Internet sites. **4**

When choosing which question you will answer:

1. It is important to consider the questions carefully. Each question is worth a total of 20 marks and the marks are distributed in slightly different ways across each question. The questions do not follow one topic and may draw on content from more than one part of the syllabus. So check the whole question carefully and check how many marks each part is worth. If you are tempted to answer question 1 above because you know the answer to part (a) look carefully at part (c) too – it is worth 8 marks. Can you answer that?

2. Make sure that you also pay attention to the command words; don't just write what you know – make sure you answer the question! In general, each question will have a straightforward command word, such as 'outline' or 'identify', but you can also get 'justify', 'discuss' and 'describe'.

3. Always leave space between the answers to the different parts of the question. This means that if you remember something later or want to go back and add something to your answer you will have space to do it. It also means that your answers should be easier to read.

4. Some candidates find it useful to bullet-point their thoughts or draw mindmaps before starting their answers. This is acceptable, but remember to watch your time.

Now let's look at some areas that caused problems for candidates in Section 2 of the paper.

From the 2009 paper:

---

1. (*b*) Outline 4 factors to be considered to ensure internal customer satisfaction. **4 marks**

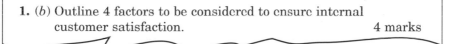

 'Candidates clearly did not understand the term "internal customers".'

SQA External Assessment Report

This is an 'outline' question, so it requires more than simply naming something, though you are not expected to develop your answer. An outline question should be straightforward. However, marks were lost here because candidates did not refer specifically to internal customers in their answers. Always remember to answer the question that is asked!

So who are the internal customers? They are the employees and stakeholders. So a good answer to the above question could be:

Four factors that could be considered to ensure internal customer satisfaction are making sure that the employees are involved in the decision making process, ✓ providing staff development opportunities and good training, ✓ showing commitment to the workforce with improved work/life-balance policies, and ✓ including internal customer satisfaction in the company objectives. ✓

> **2.** (*b*) Discuss ways in which flexible working practices can improve the work/life balance of employees. **8 marks**

How would you mark this answer?

Different flexible working practices that can improve work/life balance include job share. This is because it allows 2 people to share a single job. Another option is to work part-time; this means that you can arrange to work when the children are at school. ✓ Some people also take career breaks, where they can either travel or, again, bring up their families. ✓ More people are now opting to work from home, as ICT means that they don't need to be in the office, because as long as they have a PC with a modem, internet access and email they can communicate from anywhere in the world.

It would be very difficult to award the above answer much more than 2 out of 8. You might think that this is very low – but look at the question again.

First, it asks for a discussion – has this candidate done that?

Secondly, the question asks about how the working practices *can improve the work/life balance*, and this has not been answered at all, apart from where it mentions that part-time work makes it easier to work during school hours.

So what would have been a better answer?

Flexible working practices can improve the work/life balances of employees because they can make it easier to balance work with other commitments such as childcare, healthcare appointments and personal interests. ✓ Because employees are not trying to juggle too much they become less stressed ✓ and will therefore be less likely to be absent from work. ✓ In turn, this will mean greater motivation ✓ when they are at work and improved morale. ✓ It also means that people with disabilities are more likely to be able to take on proper work commitments, ✓ and for the many who work from home, not having to travel in the rush hour each day allows more time when they can actually be productive. ✓ The fact is that many people who are working flexibly feel more in control and therefore are happier. ✓

Do you see the differences between the two answers?

> **4.** (*d*) Outline and justify two ways of making sure employees are aware of new legislation or changes to legislation affecting the office environment. **4 marks**

Although question 4(d) was not done badly, the main comment from markers was:

'Methods of informing of changes to legislation were outlined well but not always backed up by good justification for the method.'

SQA External Assessment Report

So to achieve the 4 full marks for this question the justification was very important. Outline requires more than naming, but you don't have to develop your answer. The justification for each method has been highlighted below.

Notices can be used to highlight specific policies or procedures that need to be followed. ✓ **The reason** for using notices is that they will be constantly on display in places where staff go, and they can be produced in colour to make them eye-catching. ✓

Staff development training can be used to make sure all staff are aware of changes to legislation. ✓ This method **can ensure** that everyone is informed and staff can be asked to take part in practical sessions and activities to reinforce important points that are discussed. ✓

PAPER 2

Paper 2 has a time limit of 1 hour and 20 minutes and is worth 60 marks. You must answer **all** of the questions. It is important that you tackle the questions in order, because later questions may link back to earlier ones. However, if you get stuck, try the other questions and see how much of them you can get done. You will be given a business problem to solve, and you will need to use spreadsheet, word processing and database software to help you solve it.

One of the tasks will require *integration*, which means using more than one package to do the task. The task could be something like merging names and addresses held in a database with a letter that has been created using word processing software.

The paper will start with a brief section called *Information for candidates*. Take your time and read this carefully. It will give you an overview of what you have to do, and it might contain some information that you need to apply to some or all of the tasks.

For example, it might tell you to:

- put a specific reference on the footer of each page;
- include the new brochure with the letter;
- date the report the 1st of next month;

Make sure that you highlight any instructions like this, and put a note beside the relevant question to *see info* or *remember enclosure* (Enc) if there is one. These instructions may not be repeated again in the paper, but forgetting to do something mentioned in the *Information for candidates* section will cost you a mark or two!

When doing Paper 2, you need to use your common sense, and if necessary perform tasks that are not explicitly asked for. This could mean:

- Adding another worksheet to your spreadsheet file to add the next month's figures
- Ensuring that the reference and date are on a letter
- Making sure that the complementary close on a letter is the right one for the salutation used
- Adding Enc/Encs to the end of a letter if the body says there is an enclosure
- Creating a query in a database to extract the records required for a mail merge.

Read the tasks carefully and make sure that you understand what is required before you dive in.

Don't spend a quarter of an hour trying to remember how to count the number of product lines using a spreadsheet function if your mind has gone blank. You will not leave enough time to answer all of the other questions in the paper. And this could cost you a lot of marks, so move on.

However, don't just abandon a task because you can't do a bit of it. Work through it doing as much as you possibly can. There will usually be some easy marks. If you need to use a formula, copy it down in a column and format it in a specific way; don't do nothing just because you can't get the formula right. A mark or two may be given for copying (replicating) and formatting too – so put in a formula then copy and format, just in case.

What is problem solving?

In Paper 2 you need to problem solve.

This means that you will be given a task to do – but you won't be told how to do it. You have to work out *how* you could do it. Before you can decide on a way forward you will need to read the task carefully, so that you are clear about what you are trying to achieve.

Let's say you have been given a spreadsheet with two worksheets in it – one showing Aberdeen sales figures and another showing Edinburgh sales figures. You have been asked to *prepare a worksheet with the same layout as the Edinburgh and Aberdeen one ready for the Glasgow figures*, which should be with you by the end of the week.

Your current spreadsheet file has two worksheets – one called Aberdeen and the other called Edinburgh.

To complete this task you could:

1. Add a new worksheet.
2. Copy the information from the Edinburgh or Aberdeen worksheet onto it. (It's quicker than re-typing it.)
3. Delete the sales figures on the new worksheet, leaving space for the Glasgow ones (but being careful not to delete any formulas that should remain, for instance in the Total row and column in this example).
4. Edit the worksheet title in A1 so that it says Glasgow Sales Figures.
5. Rename the worksheet 'Glasgow'.

> Can you think of another way of achieving the same result as steps 1 and 2?

So to complete this task, you had to do lots of things that were not explicitly asked for. This is what we mean by problem solving (and using your initiative). It's not just a case of doing what you are told, but doing what needs to be done to get the desired outcome.

SPREADSHEETS

The following is a summary of the spreadsheet features and functions that you should be familiar with at Higher level. But don't forget those that you learned at Standard Grade or Intermediate 2 level – it is assumed that you are up to speed with them too.

Working with cells and cell data

- Cell formatting, including conditional formatting
- Comments – add, edit, remove

Managing workbooks

- Insert common data or formulas and formats simultaneously (linking or grouping worksheets)
- Insert page breaks

Data consolidation

- Summary worksheets/files using 3D references, pivot tables, pivot charts

Functions

- COUNTIF
- SUMIF
- ROUND
- VLOOKUP and HLOOKUP

Sorting, filtering and summarising

- Filtering on two criteria
- Grouping and outlining
- Subtotals

Charts

- Customise data series in rows and columns

Importing data from external source

- Importing a table from word processing document
- Importing data from a database table

Exporting dynamically linked data

- Link spreadsheet data as a table and/or chart in a word processing document

Print

- Completed worksheets and sections from worksheets in value and formulas view
- Separate and embedded charts

The exam question won't tell you what feature or function to use – you will need to work that out for yourself.

There will often be more than one way of solving a given problem.

'Although spreadsheets normally provide the greatest challenge for Higher candidates, "easy" marks were still not picked up: insertion of consistent style headings, formatting cells for currency or percentage, replication of formulas and printing in a specific format, remembering to add things like job reference in the footer, printing specific columns etc.'

SQA External Assessment Report

So don't give up on spreadsheet questions – try *everything*!

The following pages give examples of questions that have appeared in recent exam papers, with suggestions on how you could have answered them. There will often be more than one way of solving a problem – see if you can think of alternative ways of solving them, and decide what you think works best.

You will find links to past papers and the electronic files that go with them in the Administration section of the SQA website.

Most of the examples on the next few pages are from the 2008 paper.

The spreadsheet file was called SALES and consisted of two worksheets. One worksheet contained sales data for April (in rows 1–210) and the other contained summary data – most of which you were asked to provide.

In the paper, you were asked to perform the following task:

> In the summary sheet, show the sales for each of the sections for April.

The sales data is presented in a list on the 'sales' sheet. This list actually runs to 200 rows – so you don't want to get bogged down doing manual calculations on it!

The sections are identified by codes 1, 2, 3 and 4.

Subtotals

You could collate this data by using subtotals. If you used this feature, you would need to:

- sort the CODE column in the SALES worksheet into ascending (or descending) order – so that all sales to each code were listed together;
- use the 'subtotal' feature to SUM the VALUE column at each change in CODE.

> Remember to sort the data on the column that you will be creating your subtotals from *before* you do the subtotals.

	A	B	C	D	E	F	G
1	DATE	CODE	RECEIPT NO	METHOD OF PAYMENT	VALUE	SALES PERSON ID	
2	01/04/2008	1	1-236	CHEQUE	£12,126.00	KL	
3	01/04/2008	1	1-237	CREDIT CARD	£13,698.00	KL	
4	01/04/2008	2	2-361	CASH	£2.99	AM	
5	01/04/2008	4	4-789	DEBIT CARD	£9,700.00	PL	
6	01/04/2008	4	4-790	DEBIT CARD	£5,600.00	WJ	
7	02/04/2008	2	2-362	CREDIT CARD	£300.00	AM	
8	02/04/2008	2	2-363	CREDIT CARD	£369.45	AM	
9	02/04/2008	3	3-562	CASH	£123.69		
10	02/04/2008	3	3-561	DEBIT CARD	£80.98		
11	03/04/2008	3	3-563	CREDIT CARD	£147.98		
12	04/04/2008	3	3-564	DEBIT CARD	£369.23		
13	05/04/2008	1	1-239	CREDIT CARD	£16,789.00	KL	
14	05/04/2008	1	1-240	CREDIT CARD	£14,500.00	IG	
15	05/04/2008	1	1-238	FINANCE	£15,987.00	IG	
16	05/04/2008	2	2-365	CASH	£32.69	AM	
17	05/04/2008	2	2-366	CASH	£236.00	HMcD	
18	05/04/2008	2	2-369	CASH	£14.78	HMcD	
19	05/04/2008	2	2-364	DEBIT CARD	£65.36	AM	
20	05/04/2008	2	2-367	DEBIT CARD	£36.98	HMcD	
21	05/04/2008	2	2-368	DEBIT CARD	£78.45	HMcD	
22	05/04/2008	4	4-791	CREDIT CARD	£9,800.00	CR	
23	05/04/2008	4	4-793	CREDIT CARD	£9,870.00	WJ	

Collapse the outline down (if you like) to see the totals for each section.

Break the question down to answer it. Do each bit at a time, and tick it off on your paper when you have done it. Don't panic – work your way through the task steadily.

The summary data sheet has been started.

Pay attention to detail! The codes are not in ascending or descending order.

Because there is no column for April on the worksheet provided, you will need to add a new column for it and then enter the figures.

Another option could have been to **sort** the CODE column, and then use SUM to add up the values in each section.

- Don't waste time and risk errors by re-typing the figures – put in a formula, such as =**SALES!E41**.
- Pay careful attention to the order of the items.

=SALES tells the formula to look at the worksheet called SALES.
! acts as a separator between the worksheet name and the cell reference.

SALES worked [Compatibility Mode]

	A	B	C	D	E	F
2	CODE	SECTION	JANUARY	FEBRUARY	MARCH	APRIL
3	1	New Sales	289369	321874	399478	=SALES!E41
4	4	Pre-owned	69236	88369	140984	=SALES!E214
5	2	Shop	5365.87	8921.66	9800.1	=SALES!E146
6	3	Workshop	7456.34	7120.5	7896.55	=SALES!E184
7						
8	BANK CHARGES					
			Total Bank			

SALES / Chart1 **SUMMARY**

Ready   120%

SUMIF

Another option would be the **SUMIF** function.

The SUMIF function is used to add up the values in a range of cells *provided* the cells meet the criteria given.

In the following example SUMIF is used to calculate animal numbers on local farms.

In the first example the SUMIF is saying:

- Look at the cell range A2:A10.
- Check for a match for 'Swaney' – quotation marks are used because it is text.
- If a match is found, SUM the values for Swaney that are in the cell range C2:C10.

The total number of pigs on all farms is calculated in a similar way – this time looking for a match in the range B2:B10.

	A	B	C	D	E	F
1	**Farm**	**Animal**	**Number**			
2	Blackwells	Cow	250			
3	Torrin	Cow	500		**No of animals on Swaney's farm**	**370**
4	Swaney	Pig	50			
5	Boghall	Sheep	400		**Total number of pigs on all farms**	**600**
6	Cuillins	Pig	200			
7	Blackwells	Pig	350			
8	Swaney	Sheep	320			
9	Cuillins	Goat	44			
10	Boghall	Goat	36			

No of animals on Swaney's farm	=SUMIF(A2:A10,"Swaney",C2:C10)
Total number of pigs on all farms	=SUMIF(B2:B10,"Pig",C2:C10)

On the 2008 questions, the SUMIF function could be used as follows:

	A	B	C	D	E	F
2	**CODE**	**SECTION**	**JANUARY**	**FEBRUARY**	**MARCH**	**APRIL**
3	1	New Sales	289369	321874	399478	=SUMIF(SALES!B2:B210,SUMMARY!A3,SALES!E2:E210)
4	4	Pre-owned	69236	88369	140984	=SUMIF(SALES!B3:B211,SUMMARY!A4,SALES!E3:E211)
5	2	Shop	5365.87	8921.66	9800.1	=SUMIF(SALES!B4:B212,SUMMARY!A5,SALES!E4:E212)
6	3	Workshop	7456.34	7120.5	7896.55	=SUMIF(SALES!B5:B213,SUMMARY!A6,SALES!E5:E213)
7						
8	BANK CH					
9	**Number**	**Value**		**Total Bank**		

SALES worked2 [Compatibility Mode]

SALES   SUMMARY

- **SALES!($B$2:$B$210)** is the range in the SALES worksheet that you want to evaluate.
- **SUMMARY!A3** identifies the cell that you want to check that range against – cell A3 in the SUMMARY worksheet.
- **SALES!$E$2:$E$210** is the range that should be summed IF the value in **SUMMARY!A3** finds a match in **SALES!($B$2:$B$210)**.

Absolute addressing
When replicating formulas that reference other cells, remember to **absolutely address** any cells in the formula that you don't want changed when the formula is copied.
You can use the function key (F4) to absolutely address your cell quickly.

Final checks – make sure that:

- the formulas in the APRIL column are pointing to the correct cell addresses in SALES;
- the April heading is formatted in the same way as the other headings, e.g. upper case/bold/shading;
- the figures are formatted correctly, e.g. currency/two decimal places.

Don't be careless with points such as formatting – you might end up throwing away easy marks.

The next part of the task presented the following challenge:

We also need to find out our projected yearly income for each section – use the monthly average to work out this figure.

The Average, Minimum, Maximum, Count and Sum function are very similar functions. They are performed on numeric values. The format is

- =Average(range) – work out the average of the cell range
- =Min(range) – return the lowest value in the cell range
- =Max(range) – return the highest value in the cell range
- =Count(range) – count the items in the range
- =Sum(range) – add the values in the range up

The monthly average doesn't exist at this stage – so you will have to calculate it before you can project the yearly income (the income for 12 months). You could do this in two columns:

	C	D	E	F	G	H
						PROJECTED YEARLY
2	JANUARY	FEBRUARY	MARCH	APRIL		INCOME
3	289369	321874	399478	=SALES!E41	=AVERAGE(C3:F3)	=G3*12
4	69236	88369	140984	=SALES!E214	=AVERAGE(C4:F4)	=G4*12
5	5365.87	8921.66	9800.1	=SALES!E146	=AVERAGE(C5:F5)	=G5*12
6	7456.34	7120.5	7896.55	=SALES!E184	=AVERAGE(C6:F6)	=G6*12
7						
8						
	Total Bank					

SALES / Chart1 / SUMMARY

Or, better still, in one:

	A	B	C	D	E	F	G
1	ANALYSIS OF SALE						
2	CODE	SECTION	JANUARY	FEBRUAR	MARCH	APRIL	PROJECTED YEARLY INCOME
3	1	New Sales	289369	321874	399478	=SALES!E41	=AVERAGE(C3:F3)*12
4	4	Pre-owned	69236	88369	140984	=SALES!E214	=AVERAGE(C4:F4)*12
5	2	Shop	5365.87	8921.66	9800.1	=SALES!E146	=AVERAGE(C5:F5)*12
6	3	Workshop	7456.34	7120.5	7896.55	=SALES!E184	=AVERAGE(C6:F6)*12
7							
8	BANK CHARGES						

SALES / Chart1 / SUMMARY

And remember to check for things that might remain unsaid:

- Use an appropriate column heading.
- Format consistently.
- Wrap text on column headings that are long.
- Display all data – adjust column widths/formatting if necessary.

	A	B	C	D	E	F	G
1	ANALYSIS OF SALES FIGURES						
2	CODE	SECTION	JANUARY	FEBRUARY	MARCH	APRIL	PROJECTED YEARLY INCOME
3	1	New Sales	£289,369.00	£321,874.00	£399,478.00	£575,299.00	£ 4,758,060.00
4	4	Pre-owned	£ 69,236.00	£ 88,369.00	£140,984.00	£205,390.00	£ 1,511,937.00
5	2	Shop	£ 5,365.87	£ 8,921.66	£ 9,800.10	£ 10,458.65	£ 103,638.84
6	3	Workshop	£ 7,456.34	£ 7,120.50	£ 7,896.55	£ 9,782.19	£ 96,766.74
7							
8	BANK CHARGES						
9	Number	Value	Total Bank Charges				

SALES / Chart1 / SUMMARY

Percentage

You are then asked to work out the percentage change in sales from March to April.

> April is our busiest month and we would like to know the percentage change in sales from March.

To solve this problem you need to:

- work out the difference between the April and March figure so you know what the change is;

  In this example, the calculation is **F3-E3**.

- convert this figure to a percentage of the March sales, by dividing it by the March figure. (This is the change in sales **from March**.);

  In this example, the calculation is **F3-E3/E3**

- display it as a percentage

 You should always try to do the formula part of a question – even if you aren't sure that your formula is correct. Then format it and replicate it as necessary. You may get some marks for formatting and copying even if the formula is wrong.

	A	B	C	D	E	F	G	H
1	ANALYS							
2	CODE	SECTION	JANUARY	FEBRUAR	MARCH	APRIL	PROJECTED YEARLY INCOME	% DIFFERENCE MARCH - APRIL
3	1	New Sales	289369	321874	399478	=SALES!E41	=AVERAGE(C3:F3)*12	=(F3-E3)/E3
4	4	Pre-owned	69236	88369	140984	=SALES!E214	=AVERAGE(C4:F4)*12	=(F4-E4)/E4
5	2	Shop	5365.87	8921.66	9800.1	=SALES!E146	=AVERAGE(C5:F5)*12	=(F5-E5)/E5
6	3	Workshop	7456.34	7120.5	7896.55	=SALES!E184	=AVERAGE(C6:F6)*12	=(F6-E6)/E6
7								
8	BANK C							
9	Numbe	Value	Bank Charges					

SALES worked [Compatibility Mode]

H ◀ ▶ H SALES   Chart1   SUMMARY

At last you get to the bit that should be fairly easy.

> Print the summary sheet in value and formulas view omitting columns C–E (on one page).

- Make sure that you check the *Information for candidates* for instructions on what to print in the header or footer, for example, your name or initials.
- Print what is asked for – use your **[Ctrl]** key when you select the print area if necessary. And remember the **print selection** option in the **print** dialog box.
- When printing the formula, display the column and row headings and gridlines (sheet tab in page setup) to make the formula sheet easier to read.
- Adjust column widths if necessary to make sure all data is displayed.
- Each printout should fit on one page – so print out landscape if necessary.
- If you have put your chart on your worksheet (rather than as a separate sheet) select it before you print.

It's a good idea to make a note of the number of printouts that you should have so that you don't miss any out.

How might the marks be allocated?

April column	1 mark for correct formula.
Annual income	2 marks for correct formula. The formula could be over one or two columns.
Percentage change	2 marks for correct formula.
Replication	Maximum of 2 marks per task for correct replication of formulas and functions.
Headings	1 mark if they are all appropriate and consistently formatted, for instance shading and font.
Printing	1 mark for formula view, columns omitted, and fitting on one page.

You were then asked to prepare a chart from this data.

> Show this as a chart. Print one copy of the chart.

> **!** If the columns you are charting are not next to each other, remember to hold [Ctrl] down to select the non-adjacent data.

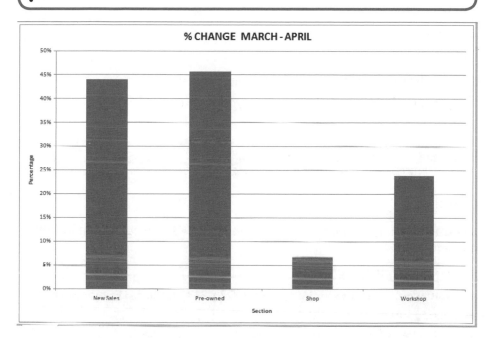

Make sure that you use:

- An appropriate chart type i.e. not a pie chart in this example. Although these are percentages, they are not part of the same item – you want to be able to compare the data.

- Titles – on chart and axis.

- Legend if required – as this chart displays one series of data only, you don't need one here.

How might the marks be allocated?

Chart	1 mark for an appropriate chart with the correct data.
Labels	2 marks for section names, no legend, axis labels.

The next part of the task asked you to:

> Find out the number and value of cheques received by the business in April.

When you look at the method of payment on the SALES sheet, you will notice that the methods are cheque, cash, credit card, finance and debit card.

You have been asked to:

● COUNT the number of cheques (find out how many cheques there are)

and

● SUM the cheque amounts (find out their total value).

Because it is only cheques that you want, you need to use COUNTIF and SUMIF.

8	BANK CHARGES	
9	**Number**	**Value**
10	=COUNTIF(SALES!D2:D213,"cheque")	=SUMIF(SALES!D2:D213,"cheque",SALES!E2:E213)

COUNTIF

The COUNTIF function works in the same way as the SUMIF function discussed on page 73.

In this example, the COUNTIF is:

● evaluating the entries in the cell range D2:D213 on the SALES worksheet;
● looking for any that say 'cheque';
● if 'cheque' is found, it is being added to the count.

Once you had the number of cheques, you were then asked to calculate the bank charges for those cheques:

There is an extra charge of £0·50 for each additional cheque presented.

> Calculate the total bank charges for April. There is a monthly bank charge of £25 which includes the processing of 12 cheques. There is an extra charge of £0.50 for each additional cheque presented.

IF function

You will need to use an IF function to work this out.

The IF function is used when you want to evaluate the outcome of a logical test and do one thing if the outcome is true and another if the outcome is false.

- IF the sun shines I will wear my shorts; if not I will wear jeans.
- IF I save £100 I will buy a new phone; if not I will make do with the one I have.
- A store might offer a 5% discount on sales IF the total value of an order is over £200.

Don't use formatting symbols e.g. £ or **comma** on numbers in a formula or function e.g. use 200 and not £200.

	A	B	C	D
1	Customer	Value of Order	Discount	Amount Due
2	Brown	210	=IF(B2>=200,B2*5%,0)	=B2-C2
3	Black	75	=IF(B3>=200,B3*5%,0)	=B3-C3
4	Green	200	=IF(B4>=200,B4*5%,0)	=B4-C4
5	White	125	=IF(B5>=200,B5*5%,0)	=B5-C5

Perform calculation if true

So there is a monthly bank charge of £25 and you can process up to 12 cheques without the bank charging any more than that.

However, IF the number of cheques processed is more than 12 you are charged an additional £0·50 per cheque.

You could work out the bank charges in a couple of similar ways.

9	**Total Bank Charges**	
10	=IF(A10>12,25+(A10-12)*0.5,25)	=IF(A10>12,(A10-12)*0.5,0)+25

Taking the first version:

IF

A10>12 (the number of cheques in A10 is more than 12 then) the bank charges are

25+(A10-12)*0.5 (the basic £25 plus an additional 50p for each extra cheque (A10–12) x 50p) If not, then the bank charge is

25 (the basic £25 bank charge)

Can you see the difference in how the second version has been constructed? It has also solved the problem, but in a slightly different way. It gives the same end result as the first example. Both are correct.

See if you can explain the second version.

> Always read the print tasks carefully – you might be asked to print the values, the formulas, all of the worksheet, or only part of it.

> Print the complete summary sheet showing values.
>
> Print only the bank charges section of this sheet in formula view.

The pressure is off again by this stage. But remember to:

- print what is asked for;
- check for information that should be in the header or footer, such as your name, any reference that is asked for, etc.;
- add row/column headings and gridlines to the formula printout.

ANALYSIS OF SALES FIGURES

CODE	SECTION		JANUARY		FEBRUARY		MARCH		APRIL	PROJECTED YEARLY INCOME	% DIFFERENCE MARCH - APRIL
1	New Sales	£	289,369.00	£	321,874.00	£	399,478.00	£ 575,299.00	£ 4,758,060.00	44%
4	Pre-owned	£	69,236.00	£	88,369.00	£	140,984.00	£ 205,390.00	£ 1,511,937.00	46%
2	Shop	£	5,365.87	£	8,921.66	£	9,800.10	£ 10,458.65	£ 103,638.84	7%
3	Workshop	£	7,456.34	£	7,120.50	£	7,896.55	£ 9,782.19	£ 96,766.74	24%

BANK CHARGES

Number	Value	Total Bank Charges
18	£ 70,762.32	£28.00

	A	B	C
8	BANK CHARGES		
9	Number	Value	Total Bank Charges
10	=COUNTIF(SALES!D2:D213,"cheque")	=SUMIF(SALES!D2:D213,"cheque",SALES!E2:E213)	=IF(A10>12,25+(A10-12)*0.5,25)

How might the marks be allocated?

Number of cheques (COUNTIF)	2 marks
Value of cheques (SUMIF)	2 marks
Working out the total bank charges (IF)	2 marks
Cells formatted for currency and two decimal places	1 mark
Printing – values	1 mark

Always try the formulas, and then format them as necessary. You may get some marks for this.

Nested IF

If there are **more than two** possible outcomes, you may need to use a **nested** IF.

For example, when grading students in an assessment and awarding A, B, C or fail grades depending on their score, you have four possible grades – so you will need to use a nested IF.

In the following example, a student with 70 or more gets an A grade, 60–69 gets a B grade, 50–59 gets a C grade and less than 50 is a fail.

	A	B	C
1	**Student**	**Score**	**Grade**
2	Adams, Peter	80	=IF(B2>=70,"A",IF(B2>=60,"B",IF(B2>=50,"C","Fail")))
3	Andrews, Paul	45	=IF(B3>=70,"A",IF(B3>=60,"B",IF(B3>=50,"C","Fail")))
4	Borthwick, Tina	63	=IF(B4>=70,"A",IF(B4>=60,"B",IF(B4>=50,"C","Fail")))
5	Jones, Alison	71	=IF(B5>=70,"A",IF(B5>=60,"B",IF(B5>=50,"C","Fail")))
		57	=IF(B6>=70,"A",IF(B6>=60,"B",IF(B6>=50,"C","Fail")))
		49	=IF(B7>=70,"A",IF(B7>=60,"B",IF(B7>=50,"C","Fail")))
		50	=IF(B8>=70,"A",IF(B8>=60,"B",IF(B8>=50,"C","Fail")))
9	Smith, Jack	60	=IF(B9>=70,"A",IF(B9>=60,"B",IF(B9>=50,"C","Fail")))

Same number of opening and closing brackets.

Text to be displayed enclosed in quotation marks.

- With a nested IF you should have the same number of opening brackets as closing ones – in this example there are three opening brackets and three closing brackets.

- This example also has text to display as the outcome, rather than a formula to calculate (as was the case in the basic IF above). Text should be enclosed in quotation marks, e.g. "A".

 If you are using Excel 2003 you can nest up to seven IFs in one function – giving eight possible outcomes. This limit does not apply in Excel 2007 (you can have up to 64 nested IFs) but too many nested IFs can be confusing.

- You may prefer a LOOKUP function as an alternative to an IF (even if you do not intend to go over the Excel limit).

VLOOKUP and HLOOKUP

> The functions that tend to cause most problems are the IF function (nested IFs in particular) and the Lookup functions – VLOOKUP and HLOOKUP.

Let's say your school is very keen on hockey and you had several teams, each with their own coach.

You have a list of the teams, with the coach name held on a worksheet – for instance, Sheet 3 in your workbook.

If you are going to use a LOOKUP, the column or row that you are going to look up must be **sorted** into **ascending order.**

	A	B
	Hockey	
1	Team	Coach
2	Arran	Swan, Gill
3	Harris	Blair, George
4	Iona	Watson, Mike
5	Lewis	Lauder, Amy
6	Skye	Peterson, John

On another sheet, e.g. Sheet 4, you have a list of matches that are coming up soon.

	A	B	C	D
			School	
1	Date	Game at	Team	Coach
2	30-Mar	Dundee	Skye	
3	02-Apr	St John's	Harris	
4	06-Apr	Aberdeen	Iona	
5	08-Apr	Penicuik	Harris	
6	12-Apr	Kelso	Arran	
7	15-Apr	Watson's	Lewis	
8	16-Apr	Dunfermline	Skye	
9	10-May	Hamilton	Iona	
10	14-May	Ayr	Arran	
11	14-May	Moffat	Harris	
12	15-May	Duns	Skye	
13	16-May	Inverness	Iona	

You want to enter details of who the school team coach is in column D – but would rather not type the information in again.

You could use a nested IF for this – but a VLOOKUP would be easier as there are five different coaches (which is quite a lot of nesting).

The information you want is on sheet 3 in your workbook, in cell range A1:B6.

> **VLOOKUP vs HLOOKUP**
>
> VLOOKUP means look something up **vertically** – from top to bottom.
>
> HLOOKUP works in a similar way, but looks something up **horizontally** – from left to right.
>
> Remember to **sort** the data you are looking up on the column or row in which you are looking for a match.

As the data on sheet 3 is arranged vertically, a VLOOKUP is used. A VLOOKUP will look for a value matching that requested in the first column of the range that you give.

	A	B	C	D
1	Date	Game at	School Team	Coach
2	40267	Dundee	Skye	=VLOOKUP(C2,Sheet3!$A$1:$B$6,2,FALSE)
3	40270	St John's	Harris	
4	40274	Aberdeen	Iona	
5	40276	Penicuik	Harris	
6	40280	Kelso	Arran	
7	40283	Watson's	Lewis	
8	40284	Dunfermline	Skye	
9	40308	Hamilton	Iona	
10	40312	Ayr	Arran	
11	40312	Moffat	Harris	
12	40313	Duns	Skye	
13	40314	Inverness	Iona	

Remember to absolutely address the range you are looking up before you copy the function.

In this case, the formula to use is:

=VLOOKUP(C2, Sheet3!$A$1:$B$6,2,FALSE)

Lookup value	Range to look up	Column to select data from	
=VLOOKUP(C2,	**Sheet3!$A$1:$B$6,**	**2,**	**FALSE)**
Vertically look for a value matching that in **C2**	In the first column of the range of cells on **Sheet3, $A$1:$B$2**	Return the data in column **two** of that range	It must be an exact match!
	Absolute addressing is used so that the range doesn't change when you copy the function.		

When you copy the function down the column, you should get the correct names displayed.

	A	B	C	D
1	**Date**	**Game at**	**School Team**	**Coach**
2	30-Mar	Dundee	Skye	Peterson, John
3	02-Apr	St John's	Harris	Blair, George
4	06-Apr	Aberdeen	Iona	Watson, Mike
5	08-Apr	Penicuik	Harris	Blair, George
6	12-Apr	Kelso	Arran	Swan, Gill
7	15-Apr	Watson's	Lewis	Lauder, Amy
8	16-Apr	Dunfermline	Skye	Peterson, John
9	10-May	Hamilton	Iona	Watson, Mike
10	14-May	Ayr	Arran	Swan, Gill
11	14-May	Moffat	Harris	Blair, George
12	15-May	Duns	Skye	Peterson, John
13	16-May	Inverness	Iona	Watson, Mike

> Nested IFs and VLOOKUPS can be tricky – and are often not done particularly well in the exam. Get your teacher to give you lots of practice.

DATABASES

Working with databases

- Use primary and foreign keys
- Create one to many relationships
- Enforce referential integrity
- Cascade updates and deletes
- Edit and delete relationships
- Print database relationships

Query

- Criteria query on a minimum of two fields from multiple tables on full or partial text or values within fields (wildcards: * or ?)
- Use AND, OR, NOT to join query criteria
- Aggregate functions in queries, for instance: sum, average, maximum and minimum
- Use a calculated field
- Sort on a minimum of two fields from multiple tables within query
- Create a graph from a query

Forms

- Design fields
- Establish order of data entry

- Set style and alignment
- Apply decorative enhancement
- Insert header and footer
- Modify properties
- Move, align, delete and edit objects on a form
- Insert graphics

Reports

- Create a report from a table or query
- Use calculations within a report – sum, average, minimum, maximum
- Modify the layout of reports to ensure data is visible
- Insert report header
- Insert page header or footer

Exporting data

- Export data to spreadsheet or word processing software

Print

- Extract/s from database
- Queries, forms and reports

Always spend a few minutes familiarising yourself with the database before you start.

Take a look at the relationships and check what data is in which table.

ALWAYS save your queries and give them a sensible name so that you can find them again if necessary, for instance: Task 1a, Task 1b. You may need to return to a query when you do the integrated part of the paper.

The following problem was taken from the 2008 exam.

Jack and Anna McLeod phoned yesterday to enquire about a new caravan. As they have a small car, the weight of the caravan **cannot exceed 1500kg** and their budget is **between £10,000 and £12,000**. The caravan should have **at least four beds**; one of which must be **permanent**.

Find all caravans that match their demands and print this information showing the **manufacturer**, **range**, **model**, the **year of manufacture, price** and **weight**.

Print the search results in the above order.

The important thing with queries is to work through the task methodically.

Highlight or underline the important bits in the problem, and tick them off as you complete them. The important information is shown above in bold.

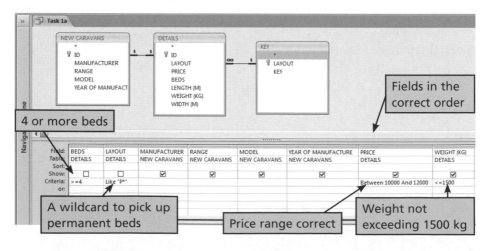

The trickiest bit here is the use of the **wildcard** to pick up the permanent beds. You really need to take a close look at the tables to see how permanent beds can be identified, for instance, the layout field starts with a P.

When you want to return records that meet several different criteria, enter all the criteria in one row.

How might the marks be allocated?

Correct number of beds	1 mark – you could also have used >3 for this
Correct weight	1 mark
Correct price range	1 mark >=10000 and <=12000 would also have worked
Permanent bed	1 mark
Correct fields in the right order	1 mark Make sure all data is displayed in the fields – if you chop off any data you could lose the mark. Remember to deselect the show checkbox for beds and layout.

Calculate and print the **number of caravans** held in stock **from each manufacturer** and **their values**.

Aggregate query

This is an example of an aggregate function within a query. You need to add the total row to your query grid to perform the calculations.

To toggle the display of the totals row click the totals tool –

'Aggregate functions (count and sum) still proved to be a challenge for candidates.' 'Many candidates missed out this calculated field task completely.'

SQA External Assessment Report

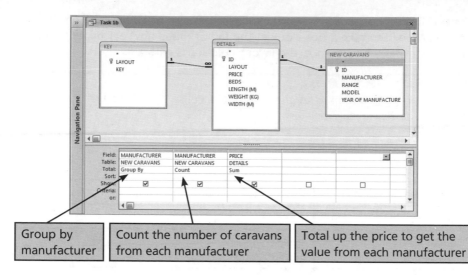

Practice your calculated queries and aggregate queries. One or other of these almost always turns up – and they tend to be the areas where candidates lose marks.

MANUFACTURER	CountOfMANUFACTURER	SumOfPRICE
Ariada	7	£85,957.00
Barclay	10	£123,153.00
Church	11	£178,498.00
Kirkwood	7	£73,177.00
Meridian	7	£68,570.00
Stellar	11	£137,954.00

How might the marks be allocated?

Name of manufacturer	1 mark
Count function to give number of caravans	2 marks
Sum function to give value of stock	2 marks

Learn to recognise and use the aggregate functions. A whole 4 marks were available for two of them in this question – and it is a very quick and easy feature to use once you can spot it.

We are considering discounting all 2007 caravans by 10% in order to try and sell them before new deliveries arrive. Create a database report showing the manufacturer, range, model, number of beds, price, discount amount and reduced price of all 2007 caravans.

Group the information by manufacturer and range.

You should create a query to extract the 2007 caravans and work out the calculated fields, i.e. the DISCOUNT AMOUNT and the REDUCED PRICE.

Calculated fields

Calculated fields have a very particular syntax. For example, to calculate the discount amount:

- DISCOUNT AMOUNT is the name of the calculated field
- A colon (:) separates the field name from the formula
- The formula is contained within parentheses: (*formula*)
- Field names in the formula are contained within square brackets e.g. [*price*]
- Operators can be + – / *
- Percentages use decimal fractions, so: 10% = 0.1; 25% = 0.25; 60% = 0.6

The **DISCOUNT AMOUNT** should be formatted to currency. In the 'query design' window, display the properties for the field and set the format option to currency.

Be careful when creating the query – you will need to include **all** the fields required in the report, not just those to work out the calculated fields.

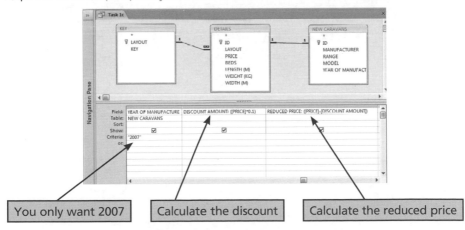

| You only want 2007 | Calculate the discount | Calculate the reduced price |

Save your query once you have checked that it gives you the correct information.

Then create your report, based on your query, grouped by manufacturer and range.

Insert the company logo at the top of the report.

Insert your name at the bottom left of each page and insert a report footer – MAY DISCOUNTS.

The final bit of the question needs attention to detail.

You will need the form header/footer area and the report header/footer area displayed.

Reports are usually easiest to create using the report wizard. You can always go into design view to finish a report if necessary.

MANUFACTURER	RANGE	MODEL	BEDS	PRICE	DISCOUNT AMOUNT	REDUCED PRICE
Ariada	Action	341ph	4	£11,980	£1,198.00	£10,782.00
	Adora	532lx	2	£10,900	£1,090.00	£9,810.00
Barclay	Pageant	Moselle	4	£12,500	£1,250.00	£11,250.00
		Champagne	4	£12,200	£1,220.00	£10,980.00
		Provence	6	£12,100	£1,210.00	£10,890.00
Church	GTS	416	2	£15,289	£1,528.90	£13,760.10
	Vogue	520	4	£16,459	£1,645.90	£14,813.10
Kirkwood	Heritage	520-eb	4	£10,100	£1,010.00	£9,090.00
	Sonata	Prelude	5	£10,478	£1,047.80	£9,430.20
Meridian	Crusader	Typhoon	4	£10,200	£1,020.00	£9,180.00
		Super Sirocco	4	£9,200	£920.00	£8,280.00
Stellar	Living	Eb	4	£11,200	£1,120.00	£10,080.00
	Nova	Xlusiv485	4	£13,800	£1,380.00	£12,420.00
	Quasar	Diamond	5	£11,450	£1,145.00	£10,305.00
		Topaz	4	£11,256	£1,125.60	£10,130.40

MAY DISCOUNTS

YOUR NAME

How might the marks be allocated?

Logo at the top of the report	1 mark
Correct fields – manufacturer, range, model, beds and price	1 mark
Appropriate new field headings	1 mark
Records for 2007 only	1 mark
Grouped by manufacturer	1 mark
Grouped by range	1 mark
Discount calculation accurate	1 mark
Reduced price calculation accurate	1 mark
Figures formatted to currency	1 mark
Page footer – your name	1 mark
Report footer – MAY DISCOUNTS	1 mark

Always check that different areas on forms and reports are fully visible. Resize/reposition logos if necessary. Adjust column widths to ensure data is fully visible in fields.

'In the report, candidates lost marks for
• not providing an appropriate heading
• not creating one field heading for staff names
• not being consistent with the use of capitalisation in these field headings.'

SQA External Assessor report

The 2009 paper gave a nice easy warm-up to Paper 2 – basic data entry.

All conference rooms can be arranged in a number of ways. The Breadalbane Centre has installed sliding doors between 2 rooms to create a bigger space. This new space will be called Chestnut. The capacities for Chestnut are:
• U-shape 54 • Boardroom 64 • Theatre 116 • Cabaret 60
Add this information to the relevant table.

All you had to do was open the correct table and type in one record using the information given.

The only suggestion here is to type carefully and accurately – don't make any typing errors!

You were then asked to display the data in a form. The form displays data from two tables, so it is probably easiest to use the form wizard to create it.

Create a form showing the name of the centre and the capacities of the various room layouts. Include leisure facilities and the number of bedrooms.

Insert the file LOGO as a header. Print this form showing **only** the new record for Breadalbane.

To print just one form, remember to view the record required and then choose selected record in the print dialog box. If you don't, you will get all the forms printing!

How might the marks be allocated?

Logo at the top of the form	1 mark
Correct fields from 'room layout' table	1 mark
Correct fields from 'facilities' table	1 mark
New room details accurate	1 mark
Printout of one record only – for correct room	1 mark

When inserting the logo, you need to go into design view and use the insert image control.

You may also need to format the logo to display well – double-click the logo to display its properties and then adjust the size mode if necessary.

Then be careful with the printout – make sure you can see everything on the form and print selection to get the correct record only.

Finally, remember to put your name on the printout.

> ACC Enterprises wishes to book one of our centres for a weekend in October. Accommodation is required for 60 delegates. They want outdoor team-building activities on Saturday and some delegates may arrive early on Friday to play golf.
>
> Present these centres in a report showing airport transfer times, as the majority of delegates will be flying up from London. Insert the file LOGO and a suitable heading. Print a copy of this report.

You will need to create a query for this part to extract the details of a centre that will meet the requirements of ACC Enterprises.

The fields are taken from two tables – FACILITIES and ADDRESS.

Make sure that you:

● include all fields that are needed;

● check the field data so that you know how to enter your criteria, for instance, yes/no field, date;

● use appropriate criteria to extract the records required.

Then create a report based on your query – you really just need the name of the centre and the Edinburgh and Glasgow transfer times.

● Insert the logo (a repeat of what you had to do in the form).

● Add a suitable title, such as 'ACC Enterprises – centres that meet your requirements' or 'ACC Enterprises – suitable centres'.

Look back through the question to help you decide what would make a suitable title. NEVER leave the title blank – make sure that you come up with something appropriate.

Check that all data is displayed clearly on the report and print it.

 Wildcard characters
Use ***** to represent a string of characters; use **?** to represent a single character.

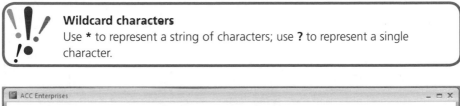

CONFERENCE CENTRE	TRANSFER TIME FROM EDINBURGH	TRANSFER TIME FROM GLASGOW
Breadalbane	90 minutes	2 hours
Menteith	2 hours	45 minutes

Your Name

How might the marks be allocated?

Logo at the top of the report, visible and legible	1 mark
Appropriate heading	1 mark
Correct fields – centre name and transfer times	1 mark

Evidence of correct criteria being used in query
    Data
    Number of delegates
    Outdoor team-building
    Golf
	
	1 mark
	1 mark
	1 mark
	1 mark

Suitable layout of record	1 mark
No duplication of records (If there is duplication, you have used the room layouts table.)	1 mark

Finally ...

> Boardrooms which can accommodate up to 30 people can now be set up as IT suites. The capacity of these rooms is 20% less than when the room is set up as a boardroom. Calculate the capacity of these IT suites. Print your findings showing only Baltersan Centre. Room capacity must be a whole number.

You need to do a calculated query for this part. (See guidelines on page 91.)

Task 1c

ROOM LAYOUTS

```
*
CENTRE ID
CENTRE
ROOM
USHAPE
BOARDROOM
THEATRE
CABARET
```

Formula to calculate capacity

Field:	CENTRE	BOARDROOM	IT SUITE Capacity: ([BOARDROOM]*0.8)
Table:	ROOM LAYOUTS	ROOM LAYOUTS	
Sort:			
Show:	☑	☑	☑
Criteria:	"Baltersan"	<=30	
or:			

Use either <31 or <=30

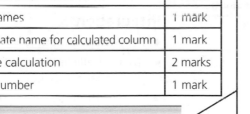

Use either <31 or <=30

Format calculated figure to display 0 decimal places

CENTRE	BOARDROOM	IT SUITE Capacity
Baltersan	25	20
Baltersan	20	16
Baltersan	16	13
Baltersan	16	13
Baltersan	16	13
Baltersan	26	21
Baltersan	24	19
Baltersan	20	16
Baltersan	20	16
*		0

Property Sheet

Selection type: Field Properties

General | Lookup

Description	
Format	Fixed
Decimal Places	0
Input Mask	
Caption	
Smart Tags	

How might the marks be allocated?

Baltersan only	1 mark
<31 within boardroom	1 mark
Room names	1 mark
Appropriate name for calculated column	1 mark
Accurate calculation	2 marks
Whole number	1 mark

If you are looking for more than one possible criteria in a field, use an OR condition

You can either enter all the conditions in one row, separating each one with an OR.

Alternatively, you can enter each condition on separate criteria rows.

Be careful if you opt to use separate rows - you may need to add criteria for other fields in each row too, e.g. in the Boardroom field.

WORD PROCESSING

You should be familiar with a wide range of word processed business documents by now, including:

- **letters** – multi-page and with tear-off slip
- **meetings** – notice of meeting and agenda; minutes
- **reports** and **newsletters**

You should also be able to work with the following features:

Tables

- Embed data from a spreadsheet in a table with dynamic linkage
- Convert text to table
- Sort lists on up to three levels
- Perform calculations – add, subtract, multiply and divide

Forms

- Create automatic form using form fields
- Work with drop-down list fields
- Work with checkbox fields
- Protect a form
- Delete form fields

Working with documents

- Create and delete footnotes and endnotes
- Modify content and positioning of existing footnotes and endnotes

- Bookmarks
- Cross-references
- Insert and delete section breaks
- Change page orientation in sections
- Work with headers and footers across sections
- Format first page differently from other pages
- Insert and delete comments
- Insert and delete watermarks
- Use, create and modify styles
- Number sections and paragraphs
- Insert table of contents

Mail merge

- Create letters and labels using a word processed data document or a database file

Integration

- Data from spreadsheet
- Dynamically linked chart or graph from a spreadsheet
- Results of database queries

Print

- Complete document
- Part of document

All business documents must be **fit for purpose**.

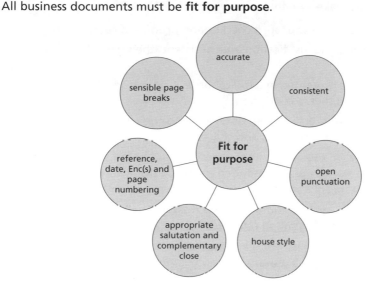

A selection of comments from recent SQA External Assessor's reports on the word processing question in paper 2 follows.

'... candidates struggled with basic word processing techniques.'

'Business documents should be fit for purpose and consistent.'

'The font for the body of the letter should have been the same throughout, including those pieces of data which were imported from the database.'

'At Higher level, it is expected that candidates will produce work that shows a high standard of presentation and is consistent throughout a document.'

'When marking the report, the consistency of font mark was rarely awarded (imported text should be changed to match the rest of the document).'

'Equally, the presentation mark failed to be awarded mainly due to poor line spacing.'

recent SQA External Assessor's reports

With all documents make sure that:

- they are accurate – use your spell checker and proofread carefully;
- fonts, line spacing and justification are consistent (the same) throughout the document;
- the information is presented in a logical order – an introduction, the body of the document and then a conclusion;
- the text, tables and charts are laid out clearly on the page – leave consistent spacing above and below tables and charts;
- page breaks are in a sensible place – there should be no shoulder headings or first lines of paragraphs abandoned at the bottoms of pages, and no last lines of paragraphs straggling over to new pages on their own;
- header and footer information is included if appropriate – page numbers, date and any other information required;
- instructions for cover pages are followed;
- tear-off slips on letters are presented clearly;
- you use the UK spell checker and not the US one.

*'Candidates surprisingly showed little knowledge of the **layout of a 2-page business letter**. Marks were lost for not using **open punctuation**, the omission of the **reference**, the **date**, **suitable salutation and complementary close**. Some candidates also confused the inclusion of **Enc** with an instruction to import data.'*

SQA External Assessor report

Following on from the SQA External Assessor's comment, it is very likely that this area will be tested again – so revise your letter layout.

The word processing task may also require you to write and add in some of your own text. The 2008 task asked you to "Create a first paragraph that thanks them for their enquiry…."

You might like to think of some regularly used phrases that would be appropriate to different situations in business e.g.

"Thank you for your letter of…."

"Thank you for your enquiry…"

"Further to our telephone conversation…"

"With reference to your letter dated…"

"We look forward to working with you."

Two-page business letter layout

MS/

8 February 2010

Mr John Wilson
15a Ladyknowe Terrace
MOFFAT
Dumfries & Galloway
DG10 9ZZ

Dear Mr Wilson

International Science Festival, Glasgow

The International Science Festival is due to take place in Glasgow during the last week in July.

Throughout the week there will be a workshops on topics including: -

- The secret hidden in the big b
- Go wireless with laser beams
- It only hurts when I laugh – w
- 21st century travel
- Self-sufficiency is possible

Scientists from across the globe will and many others.

A huge variety of events will be held will be the main venue with exhibiti midnight each day. There will also b community centres and libraries acr

The enclosed leaflet gives details of which must be booked in advance.

This festival is the biggest event of t visitors from across the country and and all levels – from the pre-schoole professional – there is something fo

---

2

8 February 2010

Mr John Wilson

The end of festival dinner will take place in the Glasgow Science Centre on the Friday evening – tickets £35.00 per head. If you wish to attend please complete the tear-off slip and return it to the above address with full payment.

Visit our website at www.glasgowsciencefestival.co.uk to browse the whole programme.

Yours sincerely

Michael Smith
Marketing Executive

Enc

✂

Science Festival Dinner

No of tickets required .... at £35.00 each. Total enclosed ....
(maximum of 4 tickets per applicant)

Name ....

Address ....

....

....

Tel No: .... Email: ....

- Reference: complete with your initials
- Date
- Inside address

Correct details at the top of the continuation sheet

Note of enclosure(s) if there are any

Make sure that you have the correct
- salutation
- complementary close

Well presented tear-off on page 2

The word processing task could assess your document layout skills using a range of documents. For example, in the last few years these are the documents that have appeared in this section:

- 2004 – minutes and report
- 2005 – mail merge
- 2006 – memo
- 2007 – multi-page report
- 2008 – two-page business letter
- 2009 – multi-page newsletter

So revise all these document layouts as they could be asked for at any time.

Report layout

Make sure that the formatting and spacing that you use for your headings is the same throughout the report. (This is what is meant by consistency in the SQA External Assessor's comments.)

The main parts of a report are usually the introduction, terms of reference, procedure, findings, conclusion and recommendations.

If the report is several pages long, it will usually have page numbers on it (although often not on the first page).

Be careful with page breaks – don't leave shoulder headings at the bottom of a page and the following paragraph at the top of the next page. (Use manual page breaks if necessary.)

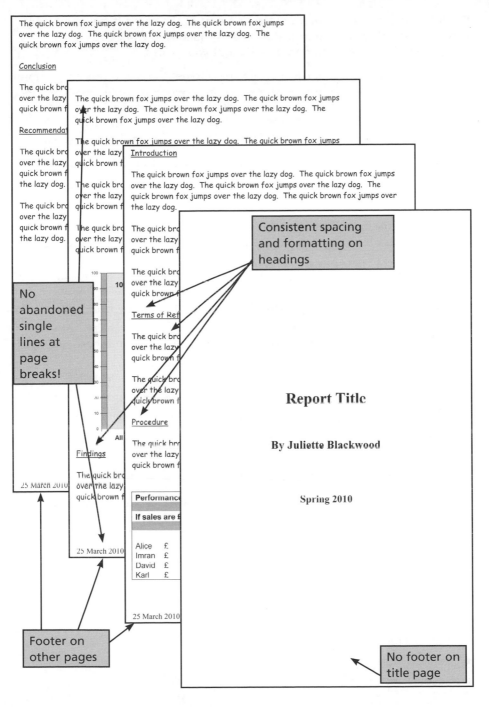

Don't be careless with the word processing part of the exam. It may *seem* a bit easier because there are no tricky formulas or queries to work out – but you have to pay a lot of attention to detail to get your marks.

There are several marks that could be very easy to get – and also very easy to lose!

> Remember that the document needs to be fit for purpose. This requires consistency in formatting and layout, acceptable house style and accuracy. Follow the instructions and check for spelling errors (making sure you use the UK spell checker).

The word processing question will usually be worth 18–20 marks – so get as many as you can.

This was the task in the 2009 exam:

> The monthly newsletter still requires some work.
>
> ● Change the layout to portrait for all pages except the last one.
> ● Create a new first page with the logo and the first two headings.
> ● The footer should show, on all pages except the first page, both slogans from the Logo (LHS and RHS) and a page number.
> ● Extract the relevant spreadsheet columns to show whether or not the Adrenaline Package is to be offered by each centre. Insert this information at the appropriate point.
> ● Complete the last page for Breadalbane using the text on *page five* and information from the database. (Do not change formatting.)
> ● Print the monthly newsletter.

Although this was presented as a newsletter, the basic layout and formatting used is similar to what you would apply to most multi-page documents, such as a report.

Word processing skills required for this task include:

● Insert section breaks
● Orientation
● Insert page breaks
● Insert picture from file
● Adjust picture size
● Headers and footers

- Page numbering (with different first page)
- Show non-printing characters – a useful feature when working on a document layout, just to let you see what is actually affecting the layout. It could be tabs, page breaks, section breaks, spaces, line feeds etc. If you don't show your non-printing characters you are left guessing!
- Copy and paste from spreadsheet
- Table formatting – to ensure that data brought in from the spreadsheet file is formatted consistently with the document
- Copy and paste from database

> On opening the draft newsletter (or any document that you are going to be doing a lot of formatting on) the first thing to do is show your non-printing characters.
>
> When you show your non-printing characters you will see exactly what is affecting the layout of your document – spaces, tabs, tables, manual page breaks, section breaks etc.

If you show the non-printing characters in the draft newsletter you will notice a manual page break separating pages 2 and 3. This needs to be replaced with a section break so that you can format the last page landscape and the others portrait.

How might the marks be allocated?

Document changed to portrait (last page landscape)	1 mark
New first page/headings	1 mark
Logo	1 mark
Accurate footer – slogans from logos and page numbering	1 mark
Positioning of last page footer	1 mark
Spreadsheet data inserted	1 mark
Columns omitted	1 mark
Number of bedrooms	1 mark
Leisure facilities	1 mark
Keying in first box	2 marks
Keying in second box	1 mark
Keying in third box	1 mark
Layout/presentation – consistency in font, justification, line spacing, sensible page breaks, etc.	1 mark

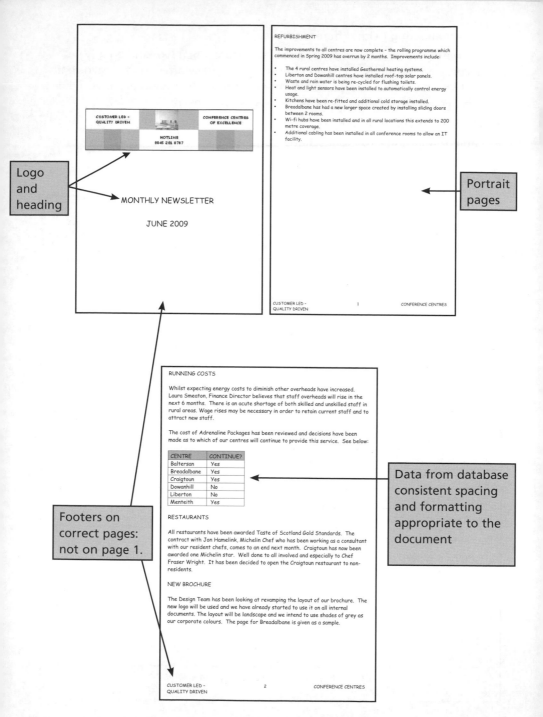

Logo and heading

Portrait pages

REFURBISHMENT

The improvements to all centres are now complete – the rolling programme which commenced in Spring 2009 has overrun by 2 months. Improvements include:

- The 4 rural centres have installed Geothermal heating systems.
- Liberton and Dowanhill centres have installed roof-top solar panels.
- Waste and rain water is being re-cycled for flushing toilets.
- Heat and light sensors have been installed to automatically control energy usage.
- Kitchens have been re-fitted and additional cold storage installed.
- Breadalbane has had a new larger space created by installing sliding doors between 2 rooms.
- Wi-fi hubs have been installed and in all rural locations this extends to 200 metre coverage.
- Additional cabling has been installed in all conference rooms to allow an IT facility.

CUSTOMER LED –
QUALITY DRIVEN

CONFERENCE CENTRES OF EXCELLENCE

HOTLINE
0845 201 8787

MONTHLY NEWSLETTER

JUNE 2009

CUSTOMER LED -
QUALITY DRIVEN   1   CONFERENCE CENTRES

RUNNING COSTS

Whilst expecting energy costs to diminish other overheads have increased. Laura Smeaton, Finance Director believes that staff overheads will rise in the next 6 months. There is an acute shortage of both skilled and unskilled staff in rural areas. Wage rises may be necessary in order to retain current staff and to attract new staff.

The cost of Adrenaline Packages has been reviewed and decisions have been made as to which of our centres will continue to provide this service. See below:

CENTRE	CONTINUE?
Baltersan	Yes
Breadalbane	Yes
Craigtoun	Yes
Dowanhill	No
Liberton	No
Menteith	Yes

Data from database consistent spacing and formatting appropriate to the document

RESTAURANTS

All restaurants have been awarded Taste of Scotland Gold Standards. The contract with Jon Hamelink, Michelin Chef who has been working as a consultant with our resident chefs, comes to an end next month. Craigtoun has now been awarded one Michelin star. Well done to all involved and especially to Chef Fraser Wright. It has been decided to open the Craigtoun restaurant to non-residents.

NEW BROCHURE

The Design Team has been looking at revamping the layout of our brochure. The new logo will be used and we have already started to use it on all internal documents. The layout will be landscape and we intend to use shades of grey as our corporate colours. The page for Breadalbane is given as a sample.

Footers on correct pages: not on page 1.

CUSTOMER LED -
QUALITY DRIVEN   2   CONFERENCE CENTRES

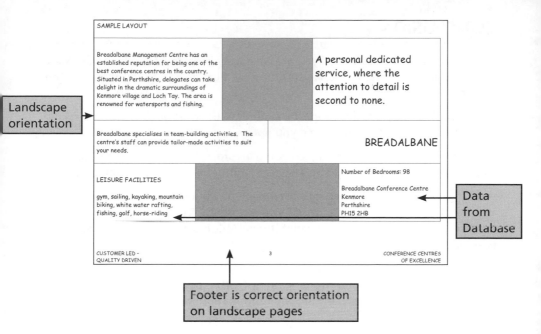

Landscape orientation

Data from Database

Footer is correct orientation on landscape pages

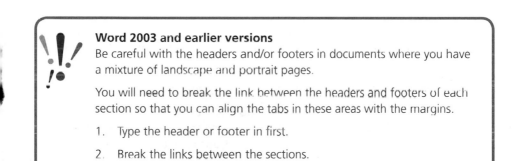

Word 2003 and earlier versions

Be careful with the headers and/or footers in documents where you have a mixture of landscape and portrait pages.

You will need to break the link between the headers and footers of each section so that you can align the tabs in these areas with the margins.

1. Type the header or footer in first.

2. Break the links between the sections.

3. Adjust the tabs on the landscape page(s).

CONCLUSION

If you are using this book at all you are obviously keen to do well in your exam and are trying to work hard towards that goal. Putting some strategies together can help.

You should start by making yourself a timetable of when your exams are taking place and plan out how much time you have to spend on each subject.

In addition to knowing your subject, you will improve your chances of doing well in your exams if you practice and feel confident in your own abilities.

Working through practice papers under exam conditions will give you a good indication of how well you can tackle the questions. The more revision and practise you can do the better, even if it means doing a practice paper more than once.

Managing your time is extremely important, both before the examination and during it. Beforehand, try to avoid being distracted by time-stealers – social networking, texting, TV etc. During the examination keep an eye on the clock.

In Paper 1, try to answer all the questions. If you leave one out go back to it – writing something is always better than writing nothing.

In Paper 2, don't spend ages trying to get a formula to work or to get a page break in the right place in a database report – move on. The more you do of the paper the more marks you are likely to get – and getting stuck for a long time at a bit you find tricky may result in you not finishing the paper.

And most important of all – **read the question before you start**.

Examinations are stressful – for everyone. Most obviously they are stressful for you, but your family will also be worried for you so try to remember that they are only trying to help when they make suggestions to you.

By studying Higher Administration you have developed extremely important skills in the use of ICT and gained a wide knowledge of processes and procedures used in offices today. This subject requires you to be organised and to work to deadlines – skills that you will need later in life. It is also a valuable subject for going into employment or on to further study.

Success comes with hard work – if you put in the work you will be rewarded.